AN INTRODUCTION TO THE RCIA

THE VISION OF CHRISTIAN INITIATION

RONALD J. LEWINSKI

LITURGY
TRAINING
PUBLICATIONS

Nihil Obstat
Very Reverend Daniel A. Smilanic, JCD
Vicar for Canonical Services
Archdiocese of Chicago
January 9, 2017

Imprimatur
Very Reverend Ronald A. Hicks
Vicar General
Archdiocese of Chicago
January 9, 2017

AN INTRODUCTION TO THE RCIA: THE VISION OF CHRISTIAN INITIATION © 2017 Archdiocese of Chicago: Liturgy Training Publications, 3949 South Racine Avenue, Chicago, IL 60609, 800-933-1800; fax 800-933-7094; e-mail orders@ltp.org. See our website at www.LTP.org. All rights reserved.

This book was edited by Danielle A. Noe, MDIV, with the assistance of Victoria M. Tufano. Michael Ruzicki was the editorial consultant, Michael A. Dodd was the production editor, Anna Manhart was the designer, and Kari Nicholls was the production artist.

The chart on pages 90–91 was prepared by Mary G. Fox in consultation with Victoria M. Tufano.

Cover art by Paul Cainto Balan. Photos on pages 13, 60, and 69 by Karen Callaway; photo on page 44 by Mark Hollopeter © Liturgy Training Publications; photos on pages 7, 27, 49, 50, 52, and 64 by Andrew Kennedy Lewis © Liturgy Training Publications; photo on page 81 © SMM Photography; photos on pages 2, 10, 14, 16, 18, 22, 25, 31, 33, 35, 36, 41, 46, 48, 51, 53, 55, 57, 59, 62, 63, 66, 70, 77, 83, 84 © John Zich.

21 20 19 18 17   3 4 5 6 7

Printed in the United States of America.

Library of Congress Control Number: 2017934600

ISBN 978-1-61671-355-3
EIRCIA

CONTENTS

INTRODUCTION

"Go, therefore, and make disciples of all nations, baptizing them
in the name of the Father, and of the Son, and of the holy Spirit,
teaching them to observe all that I have commanded you.
And behold, I am with you always, until the end of the age."

—Matthew 28:19–20

Ever since Jesus issued the Great Commission—sending out his disciples into the world with the life-changing promise of Baptism—his followers have traversed the globe spreading the joy of the Gospel and inviting people everywhere to encounter the living Christ, to be baptized, and to join his company of disciples. The Baptism that Jesus proclaimed was no mere ritual formality. The Baptism he commissioned his followers to perform is an immersion into the life, Death, and Resurrection of Christ Jesus and the doorway to eternal life.

We continue to respond to the Great Commission each time we invite someone to hear the Gospel, to encounter Jesus, and to be baptized in the name of the Father, and of the Son, and of the Holy Spirit.

The *Rite of Christian Initiation of Adults* (hereafter, RCIA) is the ritual expression of the original mandate passed onto the Apostles and their successors. This is not an institutional program but the way in which the Church attempts to carry forward the Great Commission. Times have changed since Jesus issued his Great Commission, but the call to conversion, the renunciation of sin, and the whole-hearted acceptance of Jesus who is "the way and the truth and the life" continues in the Church's initiation practices (John 14:6).

This book is an introduction and commentary on the RCIA. While our pastoral practices in regard to Christian initiation may be more detailed and complex than the biblical mandate of the Great Commission, what we do in the RCIA is fundamentally grounded in the same biblical call to faith and discipleship. Christ is still at the center of the initiation process.[1]

Since the first English translation of the RCIA was promulgated in 1974, Catholic communities have found great pastoral wisdom in their implementation of the RCIA. From years of pastoral experience we have not only learned the values of the prescribed rites and accompanying pastoral notes, but from candidates and catechumens we have learned how unique and complex the movement of faith is for every individual. While we own these rites as Church, we rely on the power and grace of the Holy Spirit to make them work effectively.

If you have been invited to share in the ministry of Christian initiation, the best place to begin your work is with your own life of faith and Baptism. There's an old saying in the Church: "You cannot give what you do not have." What you will be asked to give is quite simply a credible witness to your own faith. This means that you have come to a good appreciation of your own Baptism, Confirmation, and regular sharing in the Eucharist. At the same time, we recognize that faith is not stagnate, but is always being reshaped and refined by the ongoing movement of God in our lives. Our conversion is never complete, for the circumstances of life are always challenging us to a deeper relationship with the Lord, who is always calling us to become all that God wants us to be.

Participating in the process of Christian initiation as a member of your parish, you can expect to be challenged and called to a deeper faith and commitment as you listen attentively and observe with great reverence the movement of the Holy Spirit in the inquirers who come seeking faith and a relationship with the Church.

While the first Roman (or Latin) edition of the RCIA was released in 1972, the pastoral practices of the Church throughout the centuries have contributed to this current rite of initiation. It is true to say that what we now have available to us in the RCIA is in good part the restoration of ancient Church practice and this restoration was called for by the Second Vatican Council (see the *Constitution on the Sacred Liturgy*, 64–66). For this reason we cannot dismiss too lightly the wisdom behind the words and rituals that have become normative for us today.

---

1. Parish RCIA teams should be aware that although the *Rite of Christian Initiation of Adults* is the primary ritual book that is used, certain prayers and rubrics have been retranslated and are found in the third edition of *The Roman Missal* (especially those texts particular to the Easter Vigil). Your pastor will be able to advise you on what texts to use.

Every parish will have to take into account the age and background of those who seek Christ and initiation into his body, the Church. Contemporary culture, societal values, local resources, and so on, will all have a bearing on our pastoral approach in a given situation. However, the wisdom and depth in the RCIA speaks to the human condition in every time and place. We will all be a better Church if we take to heart what the RCIA teaches us about our life in Christ and our vocation to be Christ's missionary disciples.

The Rite of Christian Initiation of Adults (RCIA)

The RCIA is a pastoral plan and ritual process for the way the Church welcomes and forms adults and children of catechetical age in the way of Jesus as it is lived in the Roman Catholic tradition. While it is a ritual book, it includes much more than prayers and rubrics. It offers a vision of what it means to be converted and to live for Christ in the Church. It presents a series of thresholds and periods, each with its own distinctive expectations for learning, praying, personal change, and spiritual growth. The RCIA enables a Catholic community to see itself as a welcoming and initiating community. The rite invites the local community to be the nucleus within which the spiritual formation of new members takes place.

When some people first hold a copy of the RCIA in their hands they are overwhelmed—so many pages, so many words, so many rituals. The rite provides a complete process for ministering to adults from the time they first inquire about the faith to the time of their Baptism. Initially, some may feel the Church's plan of initiation is unrealistic or burdensome because of its complex structure and expectations. However, the scope of what the RCIA envisions is not so complex or burdensome when one realizes that the process envisioned is spread over a lengthy period of time and involves the assistance of the whole community. In the end, RCIA team members often report that it feels like they could have used more time. However, the lesson here is that the Christian life presumes lifelong formation.

One of the reasons the RCIA is so extensive is that it provides several options for a variety of circumstances. There are options to be used for an unbaptized adult, for children of catechetical age, for men and women who are baptized but who were never formed in the traditions and teachings of the faith, for baptized Catholics who seek to complete their initiation by being confirmed or receiving the Eucharist or both, and for baptized

Christians from other churches who are preparing to be received into the full communion of the Roman Catholic Church. Each of these different groups of people require particular attention and a process tailored to their needs.

Since the present RCIA was published in English in 1974, parish communities around the world have found the plan, or order, of initiation most helpful for their pastoral ministry. We now have the advantage of a widespread experience that validates the wisdom of the RCIA. We have learned not to approach the rite as a "program" but as a living ritual that is capable of pastoral adaptation and is respectful of the individual. Parish ministers often report how they began very simply by implementing what they could, and then year by year built on their earlier efforts. Many have testified how effective this process of initiation has been for the renewal of the whole parish.

This book is intended for those who are new to the RCIA as well as those who have experience but are ready to review and grow a little further in the profound meaning and significance of this valuable rite of the Church. This book will also be helpful for sponsors, catechists, coordinators, pastors, and parish leaders, who can use this text not only to form the parish's RCIA team, but also to gain insight by a study of the RCIA text and how it can influence all of parish life. Read this book (*An Introduction to the RCIA: The Vision of Christian Initiation*) with a copy of the RCIA in hand. Throughout this book, you will find numbers that refer directly to the RCIA. For example, "see RCIA, 75." One then needs to look at the RCIA text at number 75, which is linked to the text of this book.

As you read this book, keep in mind that the RCIA is not some kind of prepackaged "how-to" program that includes everything you need to welcome inquirers, counsel, catechize, and pray. The purpose of *An Introduction to the RCIA: The Vision of Christian Initiation* is to help you understand the spirit of the rite, its vision for forming intentional disciples, its pastoral components, its assumptions, and its ritual language.

One of the key principles for understanding the process of Christian initiation is *flexibility*. While there are norms to be followed, the formation and initiation of Christians has to be understood within the larger framework of pastoral care. The time taken, the personal attention to an individual's stage in life, the dynamics of a specific group, the cultural factors of a community, and so on, always require theological and liturgical integrity, but also pastoral sensitivity. It is a disservice to anyone making their way to the sacraments of initiation if we were to arbitrarily reduce the rite to the bare minimum for our own convenience. While a parish RCIA team exercises a significant influence on every candidate in the initiation process, we would be remiss if we forgot that true conversion and commitment take time to mature—and the work is not all ours; it is the work of the Holy Spirit.

CHAPTER ONE

CHRISTIAN INITIATION: PASTORAL PRINCIPLES

Before we examine the various stages and periods of the order of Christian initiation, it will be helpful to review some of the principles upon which our Christian initiation ministry rests.

Initiation Takes Place in Community

To say that the process of Christian initiation takes place in community does not simply mean that the liturgical rites are celebrated in the community. It means that the community is essential in the formation of new members. By its witness and its words, the community passes on its values and beliefs.

The quality and depth of a parish's communal life has a great bearing on the formation of new members. Catechumens (unbaptized persons preparing for Christian initiation) and candidates (baptized persons preparing to be received into the Catholic Church) learn to pray as they experience the prayer of the community. They learn to serve as they see others serve. They can be moved to accept as their own the values and teachings of Jesus as they encounter Catholics who live these values and teachings with conviction.

In a large community it is difficult to expect everyone to have close contact with the inquirers, catechumens, and candidates—those who are seeking Christ, the foundations of Christianity, and a clear picture of the Catholic Church. For this reason a catechumenal community is formed, consisting of catechists, sponsors, pastors, and others who represent the larger Church community in ministering to the inquirers, candidates, and catechumens. These ministries will be discussed more thoroughly in chapter 4.

The value of the principle of community is that it clearly reminds us that it is a *living faith* into which we are welcoming new members. We are not initiating people into a catechism, Church program, or some theoretical or hierarchical ideal of what Church is or was. We are initiating new members into a flesh and blood body of believers who live the Catholic Tradition and who have found meaning for their lives in that Tradition. These are the people who together in faith serve as missionary disciples in the world. These are the people who live next door to us, participate in civic affairs, teach our children, and protect our communities. This Church includes saints and sinners, but is holy at its core because Christ is its head. To be Catholic is to be universal, blessed with a diversity that covers the globe. As St. Paul said so beautifully:

We are initiating people into a living faith.

> As a body is one though it has many parts, and all the parts of the body, though many, are one body, so also Christ. For in one Spirit we were all baptized into one body, whether Jew or Greeks, slaves or free persons, and we were all given to drink of one Spirit.[1]

Without an understanding of the basic principle that to be a Catholic is to be joined to all our sisters and brothers in faith, and that Christian initiation is thus a communal affair, one might think that studying the *Catechism of the Catholic Church* is all that is necessary to be a Catholic. Or one might conclude that to be a person of faith is a private affair between oneself and God. For this reason we need to be clear that the RCIA is not a "class" but a gradual exposure to the values, beliefs, morals, and practices of the Catholic community. Through the process of the RCIA we should expect a change in one's world view that is more and more in keeping with the mind of Christ.

---

1. 1 Corinthians 12:12–13.

Catholics believe that Christ is inseparable from his Church. Consequently our initiation into Christ also means initiation into the living Church. To live the Catholic faith is to live by faith in the Church. If the full effect of initiation is to be realized, the community's involvement in the process of Christian initiation is of paramount importance.

———— ◆ ————

Questions for Discussion and Reflection

1. What role has the Christian community played in the formation of your Catholic faith and commitment?

2. How does your parish community support, inspire, and accompany those who seek Christ and initiation into the Church?

3. How has your parish been influenced by the sincerity and fervor of men and women who have participated in the catechumenate?

———— ◆ ————

Conversion Is at the Heart of Initiation

Conversion is not just a matter of believing in God—Father, Son, and Holy Spirit. Conversion also means accepting what Jesus taught, interiorizing his values and teachings. Conversion is not just an intellectual act but a change in the way we live our life. Because conversion involves a change in mind and heart, it can be a gut-wrenching struggle to reshape one's way of thinking, one's priorities, relationships, and lifestyle. While conversion is a very personal experience, it cannot remain a private affair. Conversion leads us into the world where we live our faith. Conversion compels us to further the mission of Jesus to transform the world into the Kingdom of God. St. John Paul II reminded us:

> The Church, in fact, lives in the world, even if she is not of the world (see John 17:16). She is sent to continue the redemptive work of Jesus Christ, which "by its very nature concerns the salvation of humanity, and also involves the renewal of the whole temporal order."[2]

---

2. *Christifideles laici*, 15. The numbers in Church document citations refer to the paragraph numbers in the original source.

In the process of conversion, one comes to experience more deeply the mystery of redemption at work in one's life. To experience conversion is to know personally the immense love and mercy of God so freely given. This, in turn, often engenders a feeling of unworthiness and sinfulness that calls for healing and forgiveness. The need for repentance naturally flows from a genuine experience of conversion.

Each of us knows that the process of conversion is never finished in our lives. As life changes, new challenges confront what we believe, and we have to reexamine ourselves and recommit ourselves to Christ and his teaching. Pope Paul VI taught us:

> The Church is an evangelizer, but she begins by being evangelized herself. She is the community of believers, the community of hope lived and communicated, the community of brotherly love, and she needs to listen unceasingly to what she must believe, to her reasons for hoping, to the new commandment of love."[3]

The awareness of our own ongoing conversion should help us to be respectful and realistic about our expectations of others. Because the process of conversion is ultimately the work of the Holy Spirit and involves the whole of a person's life, we cannot program conversion into an artificially fixed schedule. Each individual moved by God's grace will journey along the path of conversion at his or her own pace. This process may take place gradually over a long period of time. Those who serve in the ministry of initiation will need to be patient.[4]

———— ◆ ————

Questions for Discussion and Reflection

1. How would you describe an experience of conversion in your own life?

2. What are the challenges we face to living a converted life in these contemporary times?

3. How have you recognized the signs of conversion in the candidates and catechumens to whom you have ministered? What will you look for in the future?

---

3. *Evangelii nuntiandi*, 15.
4. More will be said about conversion in chapter 3.

4. Recognizing that we cannot "teach" conversion much less force it, what are some of the ways a catechumenate team can foster spiritual conversion?

———•◆•———

Initiation Includes Liturgical Rites

While the Sacraments of Baptism, Confirmation, and Eucharist are the climax of the initiation process for catechumens (those seeking full initiation), there are several other ritual experiences that punctuate an individual's growth in faith. The order of initiation includes the Rite of Acceptance into the Order of Catechumens, the Rite of Election, blessings, scrutinies, and Liturgies of the Word. For candidates who are already baptized, rites are used along the way that respect the candidates' Baptism but rely on God's grace which flows through the prayers and rituals employed to aid the candidates.

The various rituals in the full process of Christian initiation not only mark and celebrate a progression in faith but, like all liturgical experiences, they also have the power to convey what words alone cannot. Ritual not only gives form to our prayer, it shapes our attitudes and values as well. Ritual has the power to draw us beyond ourselves into the mystery of God who transforms us. We tend to forget that liturgy is not just our opportunity to pray to God, but God's opportunity to touch our lives with his redeeming grace. We ought not overlook the fact that the entire process of Christian initiation is essentially a *rite* or *order* of initiation. The significance of this distinction is that the rites are intended to be points of encounter with God. That doesn't imply that our pastoral ministry, evangelizing, catechesis, and apprenticing of candidates and catechumens for mission aren't important. What our experience of ritual prayer teaches us is that ultimately the process of initiation is in God's hands.

The liturgical rites in the order of initiation, then, are not optional prayer services, mere addenda to the initiation process. These rites are an integral part of the Church's initiation ministry. These ritual prayers and actions involve the entire community, and they poignantly remind us that God is among us working to save those whom we accompany on their journey to the Easter Sacraments as well as ourselves.

Questions for Discussion and Reflection

1. How does the liturgy continue to form and shape your life?

2. Which of the many rituals in the initiation process have had a significant impact on you?

3. How do you or will you weave the various rituals into the full initiation process so that all the elements in the process form one holistic spiritual experience?

―――・♦・―――

Initiation Includes Catechesis

Faith is a gift. But faith needs enlightenment. The Church's rich teaching tradition is an invaluable asset. The Church has always recognized the value of faith and reason. Over many centuries the Church has reflected on the meaning of life and death, the revelation of the true God, moral choices, biblical truths, worship, sin, grace, and so much more. The teachings of the Church, including her formal doctrines and creeds, help us to make sense out of our existence through the light of faith. During the Period of the Catechumenate, the catechetical component of the initiation process is most evident.

Catechesis is not a dry recitation of creedal statements. To understand the depth and wisdom of the Church's teaching, one also has to relate that teaching of the Church to contemporary life and events. In the *Pastoral Constitution on the Church in the Modern World*, *Gaudium et spes*, the bishops gathered at the Second Vatican Council said most poignantly:

> In every age, the church carries the responsibility of reading the signs of the times and of interpreting them in the light of the Gospel, if it is to carry out its task. In language intelligible to every generation, it should be able to answer the ever recurring questions which people ask about the meaning of this present life and of the life to come, and how one is related to the other.[5]

The RCIA notes that a thorough catechesis should be accommodated to the liturgical year (see RCIA, 75 §1). The liturgical year, or the Church's calendar, is a yearlong celebration or unfolding of the mystery of Christ. From season to season we are drawn into the life, Death, Resurrection, and

―――――――

5. *Gaudium et spes*, 4.

Catechesis should be accommodated to the liturgical year.

exaltation of Christ. This unfolding of the mystery of Christ is not a historical review but a gradual immersion of our lives into the Paschal Mystery of Christ:

> A suitable catechesis is provided by priests or deacons, or by catechists and others of the faithful, planned to be gradual and complete in its coverage, accommodated to the liturgical year, and solidly supported by celebrations of the Word. This catechesis leads the catechumens not only to an appropriate acquaintance with dogmas and precepts but also to a profound sense of the mystery of salvation in which they desire to participate.[6]

Each season and daily observance (Sundays, solemnities, feasts, and memorials) has its own character, its own message, its own special grace. By integrating our catechesis within the liturgical year, our teaching is reinforced by the *Lectionary for Mass*, the seasons, solemnities, and feasts and the memorials of the saints. A solid catechesis on the importance of turning away from sin, for example, is effectively reinforced by the rhythm and discipline of Lent. Our catechesis on the Incarnation is supported and taken to a deeper level when we observe the fullness of Christmas Time. The Lectionary of biblical readings which we use at Mass can serve as a valuable source for catechesis, including designing a catechetical approach based on the liturgical year.

As the candidates walk through the entire year with the community, they learn to make the Church's rhythm of life their own and to discover how the liturgical calendar of seasons and daily observances can be an ongoing source of spiritual growth and enlightenment.

---

6. *Rite of Christian Initiation of Adults* (RCIA), 75 §1.

Questions for Discussion and Reflection

1. Who have been the best teachers of the faith in your life? What made them so?

2. Because inquirers come to us with a variety of experiences and catechesis, how will your initiation team decide the content of your catechetical instruction?

3. What are some of the immediate values you recognize in integrating catechesis with the liturgical calendar?

4. How can you take advantage of contemporary methodology, technology, and group dynamics to communicate the foundation of the Church's Creed?

5. What does a "thorough catechesis" mean to you? How is it different than studying for a theological degree?

Initiation Leads to Missionary Discipleship

The process of Christian initiation ultimately leads to mission. While the celebration of Baptism, Confirmation, and Eucharist is a climactic point in becoming a Catholic Christian, it is not the end of the journey. Becoming a Christian means becoming a committed disciple and sharing in the mission of Jesus. We are not adopted by God to live apart from the world, as if faith was intended to remove us from the world we live in. Faith and Baptism are personal, but not private possessions. Through faith and Baptism and a regular participation in the Eucharist we are formed and sent into the world as Christ's missionary disciples.

Jesus' mission was to proclaim the reign of God. "This is the time of fulfillment," he said. "The kingdom of God is at hand. Repent, and believe in the gospel" (Mark 1:15). His intention was that we might have life in abundance. "I came so that they might have life and have it more abundantly" (John 10:10). He came among us to transform the world into a Kingdom of truth, grace, holiness, love, justice, and peace. When we are baptized into Christ Jesus we inherit the mission that Jesus entrusted to his Church.

In the process of Christian formation that leads to the initiation sacraments, the Church is charged with the responsibility of preparing new members for active discipleship. Everyone is blessed with different gifts. Parish catechumenate ministers are called to help each catechumen or candidate discern his or her gifts and to support the use of those gifts for the life of the Church and the world.

We are not preparing Christians to live their lives in the Church sacristy but in the world of work and family, a society of trade and commerce, a world filled with many conflicting values, both good and evil. To live one's faith in the world, one must be prepared to face the world with hope and to do one's part in the transformation of society into the Kingdom of God.

By a gradual introduction to the works of service in the parish community and in society, aided by a suitable apprenticeship in the Christian community, candidates and catechumens will gradually learn to make the mission of Jesus an essential component of their Christian identity.

In virtue of their baptism, all the members of the People of God have become missionary disciples (cf. Matthew 28:19). . . . The new evangelization calls for personal involvement on the part of each of the baptized. Every Christian is challenged, here and now, to be actively engaged in evangelization; indeed, anyone who has truly experienced God's saving love does not need much time or lengthy training to go out and proclaim that love. Every Christian is a missionary to the extent that he or she has encountered the love of God in Christ Jesus: we no longer say that we are "disciples" and "missionaries," but rather that we are always "missionary disciples."[7]

———◆———

Questions for Discussion and Reflection

1. What are the signs in your parish of missionary discipleship at work?

2. What are the needs or circumstances in the larger community that may need to hear the joy of the Gospel?

3. What are some of the ways we can be intentional about forming "missionary disciples"?

———◆———

---

7. *Evangelii gaudium*, 120.

Initiating individuals into God's Church and forming missionary disciples is not a program but a ritual process honed over centuries to lead people to an encounter with Christ.

Initiation Presumes Adaptability

We may be eager to try to create one structured and well-ordered process that will accommodate annually every potential inquirer or candidate for Christian initiation (those seeking Baptism, or those who have already been baptized). While doing so might seem reasonable, we already have a plan that is embedded in the RCIA. Initiating individuals into God's Church and forming missionary disciples is not a program but a ritual process honed over centuries to lead people to an encounter with Christ, to immersion into a community's life and values, and it includes ritual celebrations that allow the grace of the Holy Spirit to shape the lives of those who seek God. Rather than trying to design a program that looks more like a class syllabus, the parish RCIA team needs to be well grounded in the spirit of the RCIA. Thoroughly imbued with the spiritual insights and pastoral directives found in the RCIA, a parish team can begin to set out their priorities and pastoral approaches.

Pastoral adaptability presumes a flexibility that sometimes may look or feel messy. Initiation ministers need to be comfortable with this messiness and not try to put order into something that by its very nature has to be accommodated to the individuals we serve. This, however, does not negate the need for preparation. Nor does this imply wholesale disregard for the overall process with its accompanying rituals that are outlined in the RCIA. Adaptation addresses the specific needs and questions of an individual while at the same time respecting the integrity of the rite. It means that even after all our preparation we must be ready to rethink and redesign what we have prepared when the needs of the catechumens and candidates suggest another direction. Hopefully this will become clearer in the chapters to come.

———— ◆ ————

Questions for Discussion and Reflection

1. Does your parish refer to the initiation process as a "program" or "class"? What might these terms imply to someone who is interested in pursuing initiation as a Christian?

2. How adaptable is your parish's RCIA process to accommodate those who knock on your door a few months after you have already begun a process with a group of candidates?

3. Place yourself in the shoes of a potential inquirer. What would you be expecting from the parish RCIA team that would welcome you? What would you like them to know about you and your experience of God and faith?

———— ◆ ————

CHAPTER TWO

FOR WHOM IS THE RCIA INTENDED?

The RCIA tells us:

> The rite of Christian initiation presented here is designed for adults who, after hearing the mystery of Christ proclaimed, consciously and freely seek the living God and enter the way of faith and conversion as the Holy Spirit opens their hearts.[1]

This description of who might be included in the initiation process envisions a wide range of potential candidates. There will be a variety of circumstances that may lead individuals to inquire about becoming a Christian or being received into the Catholic Church. The primary subject of the rite is an unbaptized individual. The picture of Christian initiation given here is the complete process in its ideal form. Some individuals will have very little formal religious background; others may have been given a Christian upbringing as a child. Although people in various circumstances must be treated according to their own needs and situations, the RCIA provides a framework for ministering to many with various backgrounds and sets of circumstances. However, this should not be interpreted as implying that the RCIA should be used as a parish's adult education program. What follows is an overview of the general categories of persons we might expect to find in our ministry of Christian initiation.

Unbaptized Adults

Some of the people who knock on the church doors may be seekers who are not sure whether they are being called to join the Catholic Church. Some will be unbaptized and have little or no religious upbringing or

---

1. RCIA, 1.

knowledge. There will be others who, although they are not baptized, feel certain that God is calling them to the initiation sacraments in the Roman Catholic Church. Part I of the RCIA (see RCIA, 1–251) is the complete form of the order of initiation that is used in ministering to unbaptized persons. Part I outlines how the Church serves individuals from their first inquiry through the time following the celebration of the sacraments of initiation.

It may be that some of the unbaptized persons who come to us will already have a good sense of Church teaching. They may be acquainted with the Scriptures and in the habit of regular prayer. Quite often we may welcome individuals who have been married to a Catholic and have been coming to Mass for a number of years. Although the complete form of the order of initiation as found in part I would be followed, sensitivity to the individual's experience and needs will necessitate some accommodation, including the content of the catechetical formation a person may need.

Those seeking Baptism may have little or no religious upbringing or knowledge of the Christian faith.

Unbaptized Children

Although the book describing the initiation process is titled *Rite of Christian Initiation of Adults*, it also is intended for unbaptized children who have reached catechetical age (approximately seven years old). Part II, chapter 1 (see RCIA, 252–330) takes the basic order of initiation found in part I and provides adaptations for children. What is distinctive in this chapter is the pastoral concern for including the parents and the children's peer group in the initiation process.

The rite presumes that there will be a wide range of ages and levels of maturity among the children. Nevertheless, their formation, like for the adults, is directed to fostering a conversion of mind and heart at the level they are capable of and sufficiently aware of the meaning of their initiation into the mystery of Christ and the Church. This is not the same focus as religious education, which, it is hoped, will continue throughout the child's life and build on the formation given in the initiation process.

Baptized but Uncatechized Adults Preparing for Reception into the Full Communion of the Catholic Church

Individuals who are baptized but were never catechized and who now wish to be received into the full communion of the Catholic Church are frequently included in the parish catechumenate process. These individuals may have been baptized in other churches in the Christian tradition—for example, Methodist, Lutheran, Baptist, or Disciples of Christ, but they may not have had much or any religious formation. They are usually believers, but not active in any church. Quite often they are either engaged or married to a Catholic.

Part II, chapter 4 of the RCIA (see "Preparation of Uncatechized Adults for Confirmation and Eucharist," RCIA, 400–472) can be used with part II, chapter 5 (see "Reception of Baptized Christians into the Full Communion of the Catholic Church," RCIA, 473–504) in ministering to these individuals.

The Church urges us to be very sensitive in our ministry to the Christian status of the baptized. We should not impose more on these individuals than is necessary, and we must respect

If the person was baptized in another Christian community, the priest has the faculty to confirm when he receives that person, by virtue of the law.

the baptismal status of these candidates. By virtue of the one Baptism, they are already claimed by Christ and part of the Church, although incompletely joined to the Roman Catholic Church.

While Church law requires very little of individuals being received into the full communion of the Catholic Church, pastoral experience demonstrates that many who are baptized have not been evangelized or catechized. They may be familiar with some basic Christian truths and biblical stories, but the Baptism each received as a child may not have had an opportunity to bear fruit in a living faith. These individuals, referred to as *candidates,* may well need a similar spiritual and catechetical formation as the unbaptized.

The edition of the RCIA for the dioceses of the United States provides a set of optional rites for baptized candidates. The rites used with the unbaptized and can be useful in drawing the candidates more deeply into Christ and stirring up within them the grace of their Baptism.

It is not uncommon to welcome someone who was baptized Christian, was raised in a religious family, and is well catechized. It would be inappropriate for such an individual to be expected to participate in the complete initiation process intended for the unbaptized. All that may be necessary is pastoral counsel, an introduction to the community and its life, participation in prayer, limited catechesis, and guidance into the Church's apostolic life—all tailored to the individual's needs and respectful of the gifts each one brings.

Children of catechetical age also may be included in this category. Their formation will need to be accommodated to their level of maturity.

In ministering to baptized persons preparing for reception into full communion, we can err by demanding either too much or too little. Through individual pastoral interviews, ministers can ascertain the needs and levels of faith as well as motives which in turn will give direction to how we shape our ministry to candidates. The designated time for the initiation of those who are already baptized can be scheduled at any time throughout the year. There is no reason to hold these candidates back until Easter if there is nothing keeping them from celebrating the sacraments.

If the person was baptized in another Christian denomination, the priest has the faculty to confirm when he receives that person, by virtue of the law. He doesn't need to ask permission and the law requires him to confirm after the person is received (see canons 883, 885 §2; *National Statues for the Catechumenate,* 35; and RCIA, 481).

The support and accompaniment of the community will be of great value to uncatechized Catholics.

Uncatechized Catholic Adults Preparing for Confirmation and Eucharist

There are individuals who were baptized Catholic but have never been confirmed and have never received the Eucharist. Most frequently these individuals are uncatechized. Ordinarily they share a great deal in common with the baptized, uncatechized individuals preparing for reception into the Catholic Church. Like them, uncatechized Catholics often need a new evangelization that calls them to a converted life and a deeper relationship with Christ. They need a thorough catechesis and a solid foundation on which they can continue to build their Christian lives. They need the opportunity to stir up the grace of their Baptism. The support and accompaniment of the community will be of great value to them. The Sacrament of Reconciliation will also play a significant role in their becoming faithful, fully initiated Roman Catholics.

Part II, chapter 4 ("Preparation of Uncatechized Adults for Confirmation and Eucharist," RCIA, 400–472) is designed for these individuals. Other parts of the RCIA can also be adapted and used in ministering to these individuals to the extent that these components are appropriate and do not overlook the significance of their baptismal status.

Part II, chapter 4, is not meant for the preparation of practicing adult Catholics who have received the Eucharist but for whatever reason were never confirmed. These individuals should be catechized for the reception of Confirmation according to their needs. They may then receive the sacrament when the bishop celebrates the sacrament at the parish or at a separate celebration for adults. Such Catholic adults must be confirmed by a bishop unless explicit permission is granted by the bishop for a priest to do so.

If the person is a baptized Catholic, the priest is required to ask for the faculty to confirm.

Individuals in Exceptional Pastoral Circumstances

There will be times when, because of illness or age or an impending move, the complete order of initiation may not be possible. Part II, chapter 2 (see "Christian Initiation of Adults in Exceptional Circumstances," RCIA, 331–369) may be used in these situations. The order of initiation also provides for a person in danger of death, whether unbaptized or baptized. Part II, chapter 3 (see "Christian Initiation of a Person in Danger of Death," RCIA, 370–399) is used in these pastoral situations.

What the RCIA counsels is that even in exceptional circumstances, some of what we find in the complete order should be used to whatever extent is possible. These provisions for exceptional circumstances should not be interpreted as shortcuts for the convenience of the ministers.

Persons Baptized in an Eastern Catholic Church or an Orthodox Church

Eastern Rite Catholics

A person who has been baptized in an Eastern Catholic Church is already in full communion with the Roman Catholic Church, with the right to participate in the sacraments. If a baptized, uncatechized member of an Eastern Catholic Church comes to the Roman Catholic Church for catechesis and the sacraments, that person may receive the Eucharist when they are ready. In most Eastern Catholic Churches, the celebration of Baptism includes Confirmation (chrismation) and the reception of Eucharist, even in the case of infants. The Sacrament of Confirmation is not to be administered a second time. They may participate in the sacraments of the Roman Catholic Church from then on.

However, if this person wishes to marry a person who is not a Roman Catholic, they must go to a priest of the Eastern Catholic Church to which they belong. If they marry a Roman Catholic, their wedding may be officiated by a Catholic priest, but not a deacon, due to differences in the theology of Matrimony.[2] In addition, if the person wishes to be ordained or enter a religious order in the Roman Catholic Church, they will need to be admitted to the Roman Catholic Church.

If the person wishes to be admitted to the Roman Catholic Church, permission must be granted by the bishop of the Eastern Catholic Church to which the person belongs and approved by the Roman Catholic bishop. This is done through the diocesan chancery office.

If a baptized, uncatechized member of an Eastern Catholic Church comes to the Roman Catholic Church for catechesis and the sacraments, that person may receive the Eucharist when they are ready.

Orthodox Christians

When an individual who was baptized in an Orthodox Church seeks to be admitted into the Catholic Church, that person usually is to be received into the corresponding Eastern Catholic Church (for example, an Antiochian Orthodox Christian would be received into the Melkite Catholic Church, and a Ukrainian Orthodox Christian would be received into the Ukrainian Catholic Church). Because of the complex and sensitive ecumenical nature of these cases, parish ministers should consult with their chancery as soon as a situation such as this presents itself. In most cases, the Roman Catholic parish will be advised to receive the person into the Catholic Church in accord with RCIA, 474. This is to be recorded in the parish baptismal registry with the notation that the person is ascribed to the Eastern Catholic Church corresponding to the Orthodox Church in which they were baptized. In the Orthodox Churches, the celebration of Baptism includes Confirmation (chrismation) and the reception of Eucharist, even

---

2. In September 2016, Pope Francis changed the *Code of Canon Law* of the Roman Catholic Church to harmonize with the *Code of Canons of the Eastern Churches* on this matter.

in the case of infants. The Sacrament of Confirmation is not to be administered a second time.

Because they now belong to an Eastern Catholic Church, they may participate in the sacraments of the Roman (or Latin) Rite from then on.

As in the case of a person originally baptized in an Eastern Catholic Church, if this person wishes to marry a person who is not a Roman Catholic, they must go to a priest of the Eastern Catholic Church to which they have been ascribed. If they marry a Roman Catholic, their wedding may be officiated by a Catholic priest, but not a deacon, due to differences in the theology of Matrimony. In addition, if the person wishes to be ordained or enter a religious order in the Roman Catholic Church, they will need to be admitted to the Roman Catholic Church.

If the person wishes to be admitted to the Roman Catholic Church, permission must granted by the bishop of the Eastern Catholic Church to which the person has been ascribed and approved by the Roman Catholic bishop. This is done through the diocesan chancery office.[3]

Catholics Returning to the Church

While there may be many similarities between an unbaptized inquirer or candidate preparing for reception into the Catholic Church and a returning Catholic, placing the returning Catholic in the group with all the others is not recommended. The experience of returning Catholics may diffuse the focus and disrupt the dynamic of initial faith and exploration of Catholic life, teaching, and worship that is geared to those first joining the Church.

Pastoral practices similar to those extended to catechumens and candidates can be valuable. Returning Catholics, however, deserve their own, separate process of healing, reconciliation, catechesis, and reintegration

---

3. The Eastern Catholic Churches share many similarities with the separated Orthodox Churches, which sometimes leads to pastoral confusion in the West—for example, both the Ukrainian Greek Catholic Church and the Ukrainian Orthodox Church celebrate the Byzantine (Greek) liturgy—but it is important to remember that Eastern Catholics are as Catholic as Roman (Latin) Catholics. Although many often refer to the one, holy, Catholic, and apostolic Church as the "Roman Catholic Church," reflecting our visible unity in the Bishop of Rome, technically the "Roman" or "Latin" Church of the West, which developed in Europe, has Latin as its official language, and celebrates the liturgy of the Roman Rite, is only one of twenty-four legally autonomous Churches that comprise the one Catholic Church. It isn't that the Eastern Catholic Churches are "in union with the Catholic Church" as if they somehow stood outside of it—rather the Eastern Churches *are* the Catholic Church manifested in particular places and with their particular traditions of life, worship, and governance. We are in full communion with one another in Christ and visibly in the pope. While the Orthodox Churches are truly Churches, with a valid sacramental life, we (Eastern and Western Catholics) are unfortunately not in full union with the Orthodox—a unity for which we must fervently pray and work.

into Catholic life. For these individuals, parish ministry leads them to the Sacrament of Penance and the celebration of the Eucharist, which can be celebrated at any time, whenever the individual is ready. This should be done in lieu of having returning Catholics participate in the RCIA process.

———— ◆ ————

Questions for Discussion and Reflection

1. How will you determine the level of spiritual development and the need for formation and catechesis among those who express interest in the catechumenate?

2. What questions would you want to ask someone who is baptized but desires to be received into the full communion of the Roman Catholic Church?

3. How might your pastoral approach to baptized Catholics preparing for Confirmation and Eucharist be different from your approach to the unbaptized?

4. What provisions has your parish made to prepare unbaptized children of catechetical age for the initiation sacraments?

———— ◆ ————

CHAPTER THREE

A STRUCTURE FOR THE CHRISTIAN INITIATION OF ADULTS

There are four distinct periods described in the RCIA that mark the initiation journey of adults:

- Period of the Precatechumenate or Period of Evangelization
- Period of the Catechumenate
- Period of Purification and Enlightenment (Lent)
- Period of Postbaptismal Catechesis or Mystagogy (Easter Sunday through Pentecost)

The RCIA also describes three rituals, which serve as steps or thresholds marking the transition from one period to the next:

- Rite of Acceptance into the Order of Catechumens (see RCIA, 41–74)
- Rite of Election or Enrollment of Names (see RCIA, 118–137)
- Celebration of the Sacraments of Initiation (see RCIA, 206–243)

These liturgical rites flow naturally from the spiritual formation and catechesis that is offered to prospective new Catholics. The liturgical rites are integral to the whole process of conversion and initiation.

While these periods and ritual steps provide an order for the initiation process, they do not constitute a recipe or guaranteed formula for initiation. One must constantly be reminded that it is our personal investment in the periods and stages that gives life to the process. And it is the action of the Holy Spirit that makes the conversion process effective. The rest of this chapter presents a brief overview of each of the periods and ritual steps. A careful study of each ritual will give us direction on the ministry we need to provide prior to the celebration of each rite.

Period of the Precatechumenate or Evangelization

The Period of Evangelization, or Precatechumenate, "is a time of evangelization: faithfully and constantly the living God is proclaimed and Jesus Christ whom he has sent for the salvation of all. Thus those who are not yet Christians, their hearts opened by the Holy Spirit, may believe and be freely converted to the Lord" (RCIA, 36). Our understanding and appreciation for the initiation process would be incomplete if we were to gloss over this critical Period of Evangelization. If we have been believers in Jesus since our childhood, we may have a hard time appreciating what it means to move from a nominal recognition of Jesus to an encounter with the living Christ as the core of our being. We may find it easy to "talk about" Jesus, but struggle to lead others into a living relationship with Christ. This is the message of Pope Francis in *Evangelii gaudium*, when he says: "I invite all Christians, everywhere, at this very moment, to a renewed personal encounter with Jesus Christ, or at least an openness to letting him encounter them" (3).

During this Period of Evangelization the Church clearly exercises her vocation to be an evangelizer. Pope Paul VI reminded us:

> It is above all [Jesus'] mission and His condition of being an evangelizer that she [the Church] is called upon to continue. For the Christian community is never closed in upon itself. The intimate life of this community—the life of listening to the Word and the apostles' teaching, charity lived in a fraternal way, and the sharing of bread—this intimate life only acquires its full meaning when it becomes a witness, when it evokes admiration and conversion, and when it becomes the preaching and proclamation of the Good News.[1]

This Period of Evangelization, or the Precatechumenate, frequently begins before an inquirer formally approaches the Church. Family, friends, neighbors, and coworkers are often the catalyst that inspires an individual to ponder the depths of the spiritual life. Sometimes old assumptions are

---

1. *Evangelii nuntiandi*, 15.

challenged by the good example and living faith of others. Sometimes a faith that has been dormant is stirred up by the witness of others. Catechumenate ministers need to be aware of this natural and informal process of evangelization.

It is not unusual to hear someone say, "I thought about becoming a Catholic, but no one ever invited me." We all have to take responsibility for extending an invitation to faith, Baptism, and Christian discipleship by passing on the invitation "to come and see." Extending this invitation is not limited to any one time of the year or any predetermined schedule. The Holy Spirit is at work year round and doesn't operate on a school calendar. We need to be ready at all times to welcome inquirers when they are ready to begin their journey with us. It is also important to clarify right from the start that what is envisioned in the RCIA is not a classroom course of religious studies. Referring to the RCIA process as "classes" is misleading, and any attempt to turn the process into a class with an academic syllabus should be avoided, especially in this first period.

The community's involvement in the evangelization period is important for the effectiveness of all that the catechumenate ministers will try to achieve during this period. The community is the living context within which the catechumenate team will proclaim the Good News of the Gospel. If the catechumenate ministers proclaim the Gospel but have no examples to point to of how it is being lived, then it will be very difficult to proclaim a credible message.

The Need for Evangelization Today

We live in a society where the basic story of Christianity is fairly well known. Many of the unbaptized inquirers as well as the already baptized candidates, may not necessarily be familiar with biblical stories and images. They may, however, believe in God, pray, and even come to worship with their Catholic spouses.

We cannot presume, however, that because someone believes in God, he or she has grasped the fullness of the Gospel message to the point where his or her life has been transformed into being intentional disciples.

The Period of Evangelization is a time for sharing the fundamental Gospel message of truth and life, mercy and forgiveness, hope and salvation. This message is not an ideology but rests in a person, Jesus Christ. We do not share the truth and joy of the Gospel in a vacuum. We proclaim the living Christ and his Gospel in the context of the world and culture in which we live. The Gospel will often stand in bold contrast to the values of contemporary secular society. It is in this context when the Gospel rubs up against the unquestioned ways of the world that the call to conversion is heard more sharply. We are all called to proclaim the Gospel. The messaging does not require a theological degree. We can speak from our own experience. Pope Francis puts it this way:

> Each of us should find ways to communicate Jesus wherever we are. All of us are called to offer others an explicit witness to the saving love of the Lord, who despite our imperfections offers us his closeness, his word, and his strength, and gives meaning to our lives. In your heart you know that it is not the same to live without him; what you have come to realize, what has helped you to live and given you hope, is what you also need to communicate to others.[2]

Eventually candidates and catechumens begin to hear their own story in the scriptures and in the witness to faith they hear from others. They begin to find hope and meaning for their lives in the inspired Word of God and the witness of faithful disciples. They gradually begin to identify the movement of God in their own lives.

———•◆•———

Questions for Discussion and Reflection

1. What is the joy of the Gospel that sustains your faith?

2. From whom and where do you remember hearing the Good News of the Gospel for the first time?

3. How might the truth of the Gospel challenge someone who has never questioned the values of the secular world?

———•◆•———

The Art of Listening

We live in a fast paced, noisy society where the art of listening to one another has become difficult, if not absent entirely. Social media would have us believe that we live in an age of fast paced, effective communications. And yet with all the messages we send and receive, the simple gift of having someone listen attentively to us cannot be presumed.

---

2. *Evangelii gaudium*, 121.

In our enthusiasm about sharing our faith, we may fail to listen well to the inquirers. This listening is crucial to building that trust which is the foundation for the entire initiation process.

Each person comes with a story that has been building throughout his or her life. This is the time for inquirers to sort out their beliefs and assumptions about God, others, self, Church, and world.

Inquirers come to the Church with their own stories and needs to sort out their beliefs about God, others, self, Church, and the world.

The listening begins with a personal meeting and interview with each inquirer. In these initial interviews we learn their background, values, and motives for pursuing this process, and their beliefs, fears, and expectations. We may discover that there has been a crisis that has led the person to inquire about the Church and her teaching. We may even discern that what the Church has to offer is not really what the individual is looking for.

Our listening requires respect for each individual. The unique history of each inquirer, including his or her religious convictions or perceptions, must be respected. It is the starting point in our ministry of Christian initiation.

The quality of our listening will be just as important as the words we speak. Through our listening we extend a genuine welcome, an act of love that establishes an atmosphere of mutual respect and understanding. This interview is not a business interview but a friendly meeting between two individuals in search of God. This is not a time for judgments or an attempt to correct inaccurate ideas about God and Church. That will come in due time. This is a time for being aware of how God's grace is at work and to acknowledge that it is the Lord who takes the lead in this whole process.

While the art of listening is crucial during this first period, it is equally important throughout the entire process. Good listening can keep us from blindly going our own way and leaving candidates and catechumens behind. Pope Francis helps us to understand the value of good listening:

We need to practice the art of listening, which is more than simply hearing. Listening, in communication, is an openness of heart which makes possible that closeness without which genuine spiritual encounter cannot occur. Listening helps us to find the right gesture and word which shows that we are more than simply bystanders. Only through such respectful and compassionate listening can we enter on the paths of true growth and awaken a yearning for the Christian ideal: the desire to respond fully to God's love and to bring to fruition what he has sown in our lives.[3]

Initial Conversion

The goal of the Period of Evangelization is initial conversion, the beginning of a turn from old ways and beliefs to the living Christ, to the reign of God, and to the Church. The sign that there is an initial conversion being awakened in the inquirer is when the individual begins to question their own values or way of life or begins to sense a change in their relationships. They may find that they no longer have as much in common with some old friends.

Conversion to the Living Christ

Christian conversion is a meeting of the person with the living Christ. Pope Benedict XVI offers a helpful clarification of what it means to be converted to Christ. He says:

> Being Christian is not the result of an ethical choice or a lofty idea, but the encounter with an event, a person, which gives life a new horizon and a decisive direction.[4]

The ministers of initiation introduce the inquirer to the person of Christ through honest dialogue, exposure to the Scriptures, personal sharing, and witnessing. In turn the inquirer must reach out to Christ when he or she is ready. This may take a long time, or a growing relationship with Christ may already be evident in the inquirer's life. The inquirers will need to be supported lovingly and patiently until they are ready. And what will we be looking for? Pope Francis offers a good answer:

> Thanks solely to this encounter—or renewed encounter—with God's love, which blossoms into an enriching friendship, we are liberated from our narrowness and self-absorption. We become fully human when we become more than human, when we let God bring us beyond ourselves in order to attain the fullest truth of our being.[5]

---

3. *Evangelii gaudium*, 171.
4. *Deus caritas est*, 1.
5. *Evangelii gaudium*, 8.

Conversion to the Reign of God

Even when inquirers are believers in Christ, there is still the call to conversion shaped by the reign of God that Jesus preached. A genuine Christian conversion will be incomplete if one only holds firmly to a personal, intimate relationship with Christ but pays little attention to the demands placed upon us in the proclamation of the reign of God.

We must humbly share in the struggle to live for the Kingdom in every aspect of our lives.

Jesus did not establish an elite following for himself. He preached the reign of God, which is "a kingdom of truth and life, / a kingdom of holiness and grace, / a kingdom of justice, love and peace" (Preface to the Eucharistic Prayer for the Solemnity of Our Lord Jesus Christ, King of the Universe). This Kingdom is a radical challenge to contemporary society, and to everyone who aspires to be a disciple of Jesus.

In the Kingdom Jesus preached, the first shall be last and the greatest will be the servant of all (see Matthew 23:11). We are not to worry about what we are to wear or eat (see Matthew 6:31). We must love our enemies and pray for our persecutors (see Matthew 5:44). The poor and the peacemakers are the blessed ones in the Kingdom (see Matthew 5:1–12). Such a Kingdom is a far cry from the materialism, self-gratification, consumerism, and violence of the society we call home today. But the Kingdom is not just a dream for the hereafter. Jesus said the Reign of God is in our midst. In the person of Jesus the Kingdom is already among us.

Our evangelizing in this first period of the initiation process is not only to introduce Jesus but also to proclaim the Kingdom he stands for and to face the conversion it demands of us. Jim Wallis has commented on the close relationship between conversion and the Reign of God:

> Conversion in the New Testament can only be understood from the perspective of the kingdom of God. The salvation of individuals and the fulfillment of the kingdom are intimately connected and are linked in the preaching of Jesus and the apostles. The powerful and compelling call to conversion in the gospels arose directly out of the fact of an inbreaking

new order. To be converted to Christ meant to give one's allegiance to the kingdom, to enter into God's purposes for the world expressed in the language of the kingdom. The disciples couldn't have given themselves to Jesus and then ignored the meaning of his kingdom for their lives and the world. Their conversion, like ours, can only be understood from the vantage point of the new age inaugurated in Jesus Christ. They joined him, followed him, transferred their allegiance to him, and, in so doing, became people of the new order. His gospel was the good news of the kingdom of God. There is no other gospel in the New Testament. The arrival of Jesus was the arrival of the kingdom.

Our conversion, then, cannot be an end in itself; it is the first step of entry into the kingdom. Conversion marks the birth of the movement out of a merely private existence into a public consciousness. Conversion is the beginning of active solidarity with the purpose of the kingdom of God in the world. No longer preoccupied with our private lives, we are engaged in a vocation for the world. Our prayer becomes, "Thy kingdom come, thy will be done, on earth as it is in heaven." If we restrict our salvation to only inner concerns, we have yet to enter into its fullness. Turning from ourselves to Jesus identifies us with him in the world. Conversion, then, is to public responsibility—but public responsibility as defined by the kingdom, not by the state. Our own salvation, which began with a personal decision about Jesus Christ, becomes intimately linked with the fulfillment of the kingdom of God. The connection between conversion and the kingdom cannot be emphasized enough.[6]

Preaching the reign of God is not easy. We can expect the Gospel message to disturb our minds and hearts as we wrestle with the vision of the Kingdom. Neither the parish nor the catechumenate team can pretend to have mastered the demands of a converted life. We must humbly share the struggle to live for the Kingdom. At first hearing, the reign of God may sound burdensome, but we know it can be liberating, life-giving, and joyful. Those who work with inquirers will hopefully recognize these benefits of the kingdom from their own experience.

The Kingdom we announce as truth and life will be hard to grasp if there is no evidence of it in the parish community. A parish must ask itself, "Are we any different from the rest of society? What do we stand for? Is it obvious?" Evangelization is not an artificially scheduled period of time

---

6. Jim Wallis, *The Call to Conversion* (San Francisco: Harper and Row, 1981), 8–9.

intended to fit into an academic syllabus, much less is it an optional program but an ongoing characteristic of the community's life day in and day out.

> The Church is an evangelizer, but she begins by being evangelized herself. She is the community of believers, the community of hope lived and communicated, the community of brotherly love, and she needs to listen unceasingly to what she must believe, to her reasons for hoping, to the new commandment of love. She is the People of God immersed in the world, and often tempted by idols, and she always needs to hear the proclamation of the "mighty works of God" which converted her to the Lord; she always needs to be called together afresh by Him and reunited.[7]

Conversion to the Church

To be a Christian means that we join with other believers in building God's Kingdom. We need one another to discover that the Lord is present to us as we work to build the Kingdom.

The Church is more than a religious institution. It is—we are—a sacrament, that is, an instrument through which we encounter the Risen Lord. This underlies our Catholic tradition of liturgy and sacraments. The Church is not a gathering of like-minded people but a diverse community gathered into one body with Christ as head.

During the Period of Evangelization, inquirers are drawn to a deeper experience of the Church. They begin to see and reverence Christ living among us. As inquirers deepen their appreciation for the communal dimension of faith, they gradually begin to talk about the Church as "we" rather than "you."

Sometimes the Church herself can be perceived as an obstacle to someone pursuing a life of faith. The sins and scandals attributed to members of the Church may leave one feeling reluctant to believe that the Church is the sacrament of Christ in the world today. The Church is holy because Christ is holy. Its members may sin and fall short of Christ's expectations, but the mercy of God prevails. God uses broken vessels to convey his love and grace to humankind. To be a Christian is to be a member of Christ's Body the Church. Christ is inseparable from his Church. So in spite of the sins of her own human members, the Church is holy because Christ her head is holy.

---

7. *Evangelii nuntiandi*, 15.

The conversion to the living Christ, to the reign of God and to the Church, which we hope will grow during this first period, is only an initial conversion. During the catechumenate it will be deepened through catechesis, prayer, and dialogue. In this first phase we will look for some signs of change taking place in the lives of the inquirers. That initial change will call for careful direction and nurturing throughout the initiation process.

Questions for Discussion and Reflection

1. How would you explain to a friend what personal conversion looks like?

2. Can you think of special times in your life when you felt you were being called to a deeper conversion? What prompted that conversion?

Other Issues during the Period of the Precatechumenate or Evangelization

While listening well and sharing the Gospel message are at the heart of this period, we can also expect to find some interest on the part of the inquirers for "Catholic things." Inquirers often want to know right at the beginning what makes Catholics different from Presbyterians or Baptists, Muslims or Jews. They may be eager to know why Catholics genuflect, celebrate Reconciliation, or light candles. They may be very curious about Catholic teaching on birth control, abortion, social justice, or care for the environment.

There is no need to put off these questions that seem either of little importance or too involved to explain in one session. While many questions or issues can be covered in more depth at a later time, there is good reason to address the issues briefly when they come up. It will help to build trust. It may also alleviate some blocks or hesitations or unreasonable fear of the Church, which could keep someone from receiving the Gospel message. An openness to these kinds of questions points to the fact that the RCIA is not a class with a set syllabus to be followed like an academic course. RCIA ministers must learn to be patient and flexible.

Just as we take time to listen to the personal life stories of each individual inquirer, it is also appropriate to share the story of the local parish during this period. What is its history? What is its mission? Who are its

We can expect inquirers to ask questions about "Catholic things" and what makes Catholics different from other Christian denominations or religions. (Shown here is the annual Eucharistic procession on Corpus Christi.)

leaders? This is also a good opportunity to invite other parishioners to tell stories and memories of what motivates them.

In short, the Period of Evangelization may well be the least defined and the least ordered part of the initiation process. But so it must be. During this time, inquirers are looking over the Church and trying to feel comfortable about being with us. Catechumenate team members are trying to understand the inquirers better and to respond to their needs, and parishioners may be wondering what they can do for the inquirers. It is a period of negotiation and discovery during which a foundation of trust and respect is laid. Hospitality, sincerity, and credible witness, valuable throughout the process, are the basic tools for the precatechumenate. If we truly believe that conversion and faith are the fruit of the Holy Spirit, then everyone involved in this process must recognize that they are walking on sacred ground. There will be a time and a place for a more thorough catechesis, but at this stage the catechumenate team has to resist the inclination to turn this Period of Evangelization into an academic, doctrinal initiation.

The Length of the Period of Evangelization or Precatechumenate

The length of the Period of Evangelization or Precatechumenate will depend on the background and needs of the inquirers. Some individuals may need very little before they are ready to move on to the period of the catechumenate. A time frame cannot be set arbitrarily. For example, it would be inappropriate to expect someone who is a deeply converted Christian to undergo a lengthy precatechumenate just because there are others who need a lengthy precatechumenate or because preparations are in place for a set number of sessions regardless of who the inquirers might be.

Conversely, there may be some individuals who need many months in an evangelization period. There may be a number of personal issues an inquirer needs to sort out before proceeding further. The process of conversion may be a genuine struggle and may proceed very slowly. The ideal solution to the time issue is to provide a precatechumenate that is ongoing. Perhaps a few parishioners could make the precatechumenate their special ministry, opening their living room one night a week all year long for the precatechumenate. In this way, no matter when an inquirer enters the process and no matter when he or she is ready to move on to the catechumenate, there will be a precatechumenate forum that addresses his or her needs.

———— • ◆ • ————

Questions for Discussion and Reflection

1. Given the somewhat unpredictable nature of the precatechumenate, what are the qualities we want to look for in team members at this stage?

2. Who are the people who have fostered the spirit of conversion in your life?

———— • ◆ • ————

The First Step: The Rite of Acceptance into the Order of Catechumens

After giving some evidence of an initial conversion and a genuine desire to pursue initiation into the Catholic Church, inquirers are invited to participate in the catechumenate period.[8]

Determining the readiness for this period is an important responsibility of the catechumenate ministry. Through a series of personal interviews and through careful listening in group sessions, someone from the catechumenate team helps each inquirer discern his or her motives and readiness to move along the process of initiation.

The RCIA offers a basic outline upon which the discernment rests:

> Thus there must be evidence of the first faith that was conceived during the period of evangelization and precatechumenate and of an initial conversion and intention to change their lives and to enter into a relationship with God in Christ. Consequently, there must also be evidence of the first stirrings of repentance, a start to the practice of calling upon God in prayer, a sense of the Church, and some experience of the company and spirit of Christians through contact with a priest or with members of the community.[9]

The Rite of Acceptance into the Order of Catechumens marks the passage from the precatechumenate into the catechumenate period (see RCIA, 41–68). During this rite, celebrated in the midst of the assembly, inquirers (at this point in the rite, they are referred to as candidates) make a public promise to follow the way of Jesus, and they commit themselves to the formation process that leads to the initiation sacraments. The Church in turn promises to support the inquirers, now called catechumens, and to help them know and follow Christ.

At the entrance to the church the catechumens are marked with the Sign of the Cross. With this ancient sign they are claimed for Christ. They must learn to carry the cross throughout their lives. By signing the

---

8. An outline of the ritual is found on page 92.
9. RCIA, 42.

candidates on several of the senses, there is a clear message that accepting the cross is not just the sign of an intellectual assent, but acceptance of the cross in every aspect of life. The community must help the catechumens to understand the cross not as a sign of defeat but as the Christian's sign of hope and life.

The catechumens are then invited into the assembly to hear the proclamation of the Scriptures. The Word of God is the foundation upon which the catechumenate is built. During this rite the catechumens may receive a copy of the Scriptures as a reminder that they are to build their lives upon the living Word of God.

After the assembly prays for the new catechumens, they are led to another place where they continue their reflection upon the Word of God. Because they are not yet able to share at the Eucharistic table, their dismissal from the assembly is an invitation to be fed by the presence of the Lord in the Sacred Scriptures. Ordinarily the catechumens will be dismissed in this fashion each time the full assembly gathers for Mass.

The Rite of Acceptance into the Order of Catechumens can be celebrated any time there are inquirers ready to take this step. The rite may be celebrated more than once in the year.

Once the inquirers have been accepted into the order of catechumens through this rite, they are considered part of the household of Christ (see RCIA, 47). Their initial conversion and their desire to pursue a thorough formation in preparation for the sacraments of initiation already give them a place within the Church. Embraced by the Church, they are supported by prayers, blessings, and other rites. They are entitled to celebrate their Marriages in the Church; should someone die as a catechumen, he or she receives a Christian burial.

———— • ◆ • ————

Questions for Reflection and Discussion

1. The Rite of Acceptance into the Order of Catechumens is usually very moving. Why do you think that is so?

2. How might the congregation be affected by this rite?

———— • ◆ • ————

Rite of Welcoming the [Baptized] Candidates

For those inquirers who are baptized, there is an optional Rite of Welcoming the Candidates, which is inspired by the Rite of Acceptance into the Order of Catechumens.[10] The Rite of Welcoming the Candidates (see RCIA, 411–433) recognizes that these individuals have already been baptized:

> Now the church surrounds them with special care and support as they prepare to be sealed with the gift of the Spirit in confirmation and take their place at the banquet table of Christ's sacrifice.[11]

The candidates' participation in the rite is an acknowledgment on their part that God has been at work in their lives and that they are eager to deepen their commitment to Christ and his Gospel. The prayers in the Rite of Welcoming the Candidates capture the spirit of what lies ahead for the candidates: "That these candidates may come to a deeper appreciation of the gift of their baptism, which joined them to Christ . . ." (RCIA, 430).

To avoid any confusion with those who are unbaptized and becoming catechumens on their way to Baptism, it would be advisable to celebrate the Rite of Welcoming the Candidates (already baptized) at another liturgy. As stated in the rite: "Anything that would equate candidates for reception with those who are catechumens is to be absolutely avoided" (RCIA, 477).

————— ◆ —————

Questions for Discussion and Reflection

1. Why do you think a baptized candidate would find this rite appealing and rewarding?

2. How would you make sure the candidate does not overlook the importance of his/her Baptism?

————— ◆ —————

---

10. An outline of the rite is found on page 93.
11. RCIA, 412.

Period of the Catechumenate

The RCIA outlines four primary means by which the Church fosters the conversion and Christian formation of catechumens and candidates (see RCIA, 75):

- a suitable catechesis accommodated to the liturgical year
- becoming familiar with the Christian way of life by the example and support of the community
- the celebration of liturgical rites
- apprenticeship in the apostolic life and mission of the Church

Catechesis for Catechumens (RCIA, 75 §1)

The order of initiation describes a catechesis that is thorough and helps the catechumens and candidates reach a profound sense of the mystery of salvation. This catechesis is offered by priests, deacons, catechists, and others in the community, who by sharing the living faith of the Church help to enlighten the faith of catechumens and candidates.

The purpose of the catechesis is not to form theologians or Church historians but to form men and women in the wisdom and tradition of the Church in a way that gives reason to faith and enables them to live by faith in the midst of the world.

Catechesis helps catechumens and candidates find meaning in their own experiences of life. By our sharing in the richness of our biblical and doctrinal heritage, they are gradually helped to value the Catholic tradition which they will claim as their own.

Catechesis during this period is not merely doctrinal instruction. While the doctrine of the Church must be communicated, it is essential that catechumens learn what the Church's teachings mean for their lives in relationship to God and in relationship with the Church community. Our hope is to lead them to a deeper sense of the mystery of God in every aspect of our lives. As the RCIA states:

This catechesis leads the catechumens not only to an appropriate acquaintance with dogmas and precepts but also to a profound sense of the mystery of salvation in which they desire to participate.[12]

What this means is that their exposure to Christian doctrine should help them to identify how the Paschal Mystery is at work in their life. While the fundamentals of Catholic doctrine are to be communicated, the paradigm of "classroom instruction" does not adequately fulfill what should be happening in this Period of the Catechumenate. Pope Francis helps us to understand the right perspective on teaching doctrine:

> Pastoral ministry in a missionary style is not obsessed with the disjointed transmission of a multitude of doctrines to be insistently imposed. When we adopt a pastoral goal and a missionary style which would actually reach everyone without exception or exclusion, the message has to concentrate on the essentials, on what is most beautiful, most grand, most appealing and at the same time most necessary. The message is simplified, while losing none of its depth and truth, and thus becomes all the more forceful and convincing.[13]

The methods of catechesis used during this time must respect the way adults learn. Catechists and other initiation ministers must keep the purpose of the catechumenate in mind and remember that growth and development in the Christian life is a lifelong process. The *National Directory for Catechesis* summarizes the purpose of catechesis:

> The object of catechesis is communion with Jesus Christ. Catechesis leads people to enter the mystery of Christ, to encounter him, and to discover themselves and the meaning of their lives in him.[14]

Questions for Discussion and Reflection

1. What is your understanding of catechesis as a path to discovering a "profound sense of the mystery of salvation" (RCIA, 75 §1)?

2. How do you differentiate between catechesis that leads to awe rather than just fact learning?

---

12. RCIA, 75 §1.
13. *Evangelii gaudium*, 35.
14. *National Directory for Catechesis*, chapter 19, part B.

3. How up-to-date is your RCIA ministry with adult learning methods?

————————•◆•————————

Catechesis Accommodated to the Liturgical Year (RCIA, 75 §1)

Because catechesis during the catechumenate is based both on the Church's teachings and traditions and on the catechumens' experiences, no book, class syllabus, or set lesson plan can be created to suit the needs of every catechumenate group or every catechumen.

One of the most effective means of catechesis during this period is to follow the rhythm of the liturgical year. In this model one can use the Lectionary, the prayers of the Mass, and the customs of the liturgical year as the ground upon which a solid, doctrinal catechesis is built. In practice this means that after the catechumens and candidates have had the opportunity to hear and reflect upon the Word of God on Sunday, a catechist will lead them to discover the basic Catholic teachings contained, implied, or suggested in the Scriptures of the feast, season, or Sunday being celebrated. This enables the catechumens and candidates to see how Church teaching is rooted in the Scripture and Liturgy. This method also teaches them how to use the Scriptures as an ongoing font for spiritual growth and the liturgy of the Church as the foundation for all Christian spirituality.

This method also introduces the catechumens and candidates into the rhythm and grace of the liturgical year. Keeping the Lord's Day holy and observing the feasts and the remembrance of the saints unfolds the profound mystery of Christ day by day.

Christian initiation teams who are not acquainted with the potential of the liturgical year for catechesis may be skeptical about how this method will ensure a thorough exposure to the Catholic faith. The fullness of our faith is presented to us though the course of the year. There are a growing number of resources that have become available to assist catechists. As the team progresses through the year and becomes aware of key beliefs that have not been presented, there is no reason why catechesis that is rooted in the liturgical year cannot be done.

A liturgically based catechesis has great merit and is very adaptable to a year-round catechumenate process, but it is not the only method. Some diversity in approach may be helpful and welcomed by the candidates and catechumens. We need to remember that the purpose of the Period of the

Catechumenate is not to prepare candidates and catechumens for a theological degree but to help guide them toward a more enlightened and strengthened faith.

Becoming Familiar with the Christian Way of Life (RCIA, 75 §2)

Catechumens and candidates need the support and living witness of the community in addition to catechetical formation. By meeting and getting to know mature Catholics, catechumens and candidates will learn how Catholic tradition, values, and customs are lived day by day. By interacting with members of the community, catechumens and candidates will be exposed to various expressions of Catholic spirituality, styles of personal prayer, family customs, and ethnic traditions. There is a great deal of diversity within the unity of the Church. Catechumens and candidates should be given the opportunity to appreciate the full Catholic experience.

A welcoming community provides an environment that allows catechumens and candidates to explore the richness of the Christian tradition as they gradually apply it to themselves and accept it as their own. Welcoming catechumens and candidates by offering hospitality, support, and good example supports the truth that we initiate people not into a theological abstraction but into the living Body of Christ, the community of faith. The community's interaction and involvement with catechumens and candidates enables this principle to come alive.

The faith and witness of a friend, coworker, or family member is most often what first led the catechumen or candidate to investigate the Christian life. The community builds on that experience. For those who come from a background that is unsupportive or even hostile to Christian life, the care of the community will be crucial. The vitality of a parish where the liturgy is prayerful and engaging, and where a sense of mission is evident, will naturally inspire and invite candidates and catechumens to be a part of the community's life.

There is, of course, no program for how a community will interact with catechumens and candidates. While catechumenal teams may provide opportunities for catechumens and candidates to meet other Catholics within the catechumenal sessions, interaction with the community ought to be encouraged beyond the catechumenal circle. Parish social events, for example, are great opportunities for catechumens and candidates to meet other Catholics. Parish adult education opportunities—for example, a presentation on Christian parenting offered by the religious education

ministries, a senior club's outing, a town hall meeting, or devotional offer-
ings can also be beneficial to the candidate's or catechumen's introduction
to Catholic life. Sponsors should be encouraged to introduce catechumens
and candidates to various members of the community. The sponsor or a
team member might ask someone to accompany a catechumen to a meeting
or prayer service that the catechumen or candidate might be hesitant to
attend alone. We should not forget opportunities to experience Catholic
life beyond the parish. Quite often the diocese may have planned a special
event or perhaps a neighboring parish or group of parishes might be offering a march for life, a retreat day, or even just a summer festival that would
be worth dropping in on.

―――――――・◆・―――――――

Questions for Discussion and Reflection

1. How is RCIA, paragraph 75 §2, just as relevant to a parish as
   to the catechumenal community (that is, how is the parish
   part of the catechumenal community)?

2. What are the opportunities in your parish for parishioners
   to interact with catechumens and candidates?

3. How can the presence of catechumens in a parish
   contribute to parish vitality?

―――――――・◆・―――――――

The Celebration of Liturgical Rites (RCIA, 75 §3)

Another component of the catechumenate period is participation in the
Church's liturgical life. Liturgy is not simply one thing among many that
a community does. The Church teaches us that "the liturgy is the summit
toward which the activity of the Church is directed; at the same time it is
the fount from which all the Church's power flows" (*Constitution on the
Sacred Liturgy*, 10). In the liturgy we encounter the living Christ, the revelation of God, the source of our strength for living the Christian life. We
bring to the liturgy all that we are and all that we try to do in the Lord's
name. At this summit where we join our daily sacrifices to Christ's, we and
our world are transformed.

The liturgy is also the Church's creed. We pray what we believe. Over the course of a lifetime the liturgy shapes our minds and hearts individually and collectively.

Because the liturgy is so essential to the Church's identity, it is important to introduce candidates and catechumens to the liturgical life of the Church. By participating in various rites and liturgical experiences, the catechumens and candidates will gain an appreciation for the Church's liturgy, but, more importantly, they will be formed by what they pray. Teaching candidates and catechumens how to pray the liturgy is an essential component of their catechesis and formation.

Teaching candidates and catechumens to pray the liturgy is essential to their formation.

Prompted by the Holy Spirit they need to learn how to pray not only "to Christ" but "with Christ" in the communion of believers.

The Liturgy of the Word is the primary liturgy for catechumens and candidates. In the Liturgy of the Word, they will experience the presence of Christ in the proclamation of Scripture. Week by week and year by year the catechumens and candidates—and all Christians—are called to make the Scriptures the foundation of their lives. A Liturgy of the Word may also be a suitable context for catechesis to take place. The RCIA provides an outline for celebrations of the Word of God apart from the celebration of the Eucharist (see 81–89).

The liturgical rites outlined in the RCIA are not optional or chosen arbitrarily for the sake of adding variety to the process. These rites mark transitions between stages of growth in the Christian life. Good ritual communicates the mystery of Christ in ways that words alone unable to do. God is always at work in the liturgy sanctifying us and forming us into "a chosen race, a royal priesthood, a holy nation, a people of his own" (1 Peter 2:9).

Among these minor rites provided in the RCIA are

- Blessings (see 95–97)
- Minor exorcisms (see 90–94)
- Anointing with the oil of catechumens (see 98–103)
- Presentations of the Creed and Lord's Prayer (see 104–105)

All of these rites surround the catechumens and candidates with the prayer, love, and support of the Church. The liturgical rites should be linked to the catechetical formation so that prayer, ritual, and Scripture are understood as part of a holistic process of initiation into the mystery of Christ and flow from and are linked to catechesis, which in turn can build upon the rites that have been celebrated. Teaching candidates and catechumens to pray the liturgy is essential to their formation.

Many catechumenate teams place great emphasis on spontaneous shared prayer or devotional prayer during the time of formation. This is a good practice, but care ought to be taken not to neglect liturgical prayer. The liturgy of the Church is the basic source of spiritual life. After the sacraments of initiation have been celebrated, catechumens and candidates may not have a small community like the catechumenate to pray and share with, but they will always have the Church's liturgy to guide them.

The task, then, is to help catechumens and candidates learn how to make the liturgy their own prayer. If we do this, we will have given the gift that enables them constant growth in faith. Catechumens and candidates ought to be introduced gradually to the many facets of Catholic prayer and ritual, including the feasts and seasons (liturgical year), and to be shown how to carry into their homes practices associated with the liturgical year, the commemoration of the saints, and the Liturgy of the Hours. They should be assisted in learning how to make liturgical words, songs, and gestures true prayers of the heart.

―――――――――◆◆―――――――――

Questions for Discussion and Reflection

1. How is your Catholic congregation catechized about the meaning and significance of the various rites?

2. How are the blessings (see RCIA, 95–97) incorporated into your parish's RCIA sessions?

―――――――――◆◆―――――――――

Apprenticeship in the Apostolic Life and Mission of the Church (RCIA, 75 §4)

The formation of catechumens and candidates should lead them to work actively with others to spread the Gospel and build the Kingdom of God. This expectation flows from the Church's understanding that Baptism and

Confirmation closely join us to the ministry of Jesus and that the Eucharist compels us to break the bread of our lives for others in memory of Christ. Pope Francis has spoken very strongly about the call of the baptized to share in the mission of Christ.

> In virtue of their baptism, all the members of the People of God have become missionary disciples (cf. Matthew 28:19). . . . Every Christian is challenged, here and now, to be actively engaged in evangelization; indeed, anyone who has truly experienced God's saving love does not need much time or lengthy training to go out and proclaim that love. Every Christian is a missionary to the extent that he or she has encountered the love of God in Christ Jesus: we no longer say that we are "disciples" and "missionaries," but rather that we are always "missionary disciples." [15]

In the recent past, the Church may not have paid adequate attention to the call to missionary discipleship that flows from Baptism. Baptism most often was understood almost exclusively as something done for an individual's personal salvation. This is true, of course, but is too limited a definition of Baptism. Baptism as commitment to service in Jesus' name has not often been preached or taught with the needed emphasis. If we understand that our mandate as ministers of Christian initiation is not just to initiate someone into the parish, but also into the mission field with Christ, our whole formation process in the catechumenate may look quite different. By introducing the catechumens and candidates into the apostolic life of the Church, our practice of initiation strikes a better balance between the personal spiritual benefit of Baptism and the call to missionary discipleship.

Through the sacraments of initiation, we are conformed to Christ as his disciples and sent into the world to further the reign of God.

Catechumens best learn what it means to serve from those who are already engaged in Christian service. A good understanding of the assumptions and dynamics of the RCIA will lead us to review the apostolic life of our parish. We may sadly conclude that our parish's mission identity is not strong enough to inspire and apprentice candidates and catechumens for mission. This is a good example of how the RCIA can bring new life to a parish community.

---

15. *Evangelii gaudium*, 120.

A sense of mission and service in the name of Jesus is not limited to liturgical ministries exercised in the sanctuary or other volunteer ministries in the parish. The world is the Christian's sanctuary, and it is in the world that we are called to build God's Kingdom. Catechumenate teams need to witness and join others in Christian service beyond the parish. Men and women involved in visiting the sick and the imprisoned, or in caring for the elderly and the poor—and others, too, who understand their mission as Christians in quite ordinary ways—are the people catechumens and candidates need to meet and learn from. The Christian vocation must be exercised beyond the parish center: in businesses and neighborhoods, schools, and social and political arenas. The resources of the diocese, a Catholic Worker House, a local food bank or soup kitchen, the Bread for the World movement, Pax Christi and other such groups could be drawn on for suggestions; these groups may even welcome catechumens and candidates to join them in their work. Pope John Paul II's exhortation to the laity, *Christifideles laici,* is valuable in understanding the role of the baptized Christian in the world:

The Christian vocation must be exercised beyond the parish center: in businesses and neighborhoods, schools, and social and political arenas.

The images taken from the gospel of salt, light and leaven, although indiscriminately applicable to all Jesus' disciples, are specifically applied to the lay faithful. They are particularly meaningful images because they speak not only of the deep involvement and the full participation of the lay faithful in the affairs of the earth, the world and the human community, but also and above all, they tell of the radical newness and unique character of an involvement and participation which has as its purpose the spreading of the Gospel that brings salvation.[16]

The mark of a healthy parish is that it doesn't turn inward or become absorbed with its own internal issues. A vital Catholic parish looks beyond

16. *Christifideles laici,* 15.

its own campus and beyond the rolls of registered parishioners to see how and where it can have a positive effect on society. A healthy parish reaches out into the wider community where hope and mercy may be wanting. For this reason candidates and catechumens have to be led into the larger field of business and civic affairs, places where the social teaching of the Church would call us to make a difference, to transform society by the light of the Gospel.

Questions for Discussion and Reflection

1. What is the difference between volunteerism (or service hours) and missionary discipleship?

2. How can catechumens and candidates be introduced to mission in your parish?

3. Sharing in the mission of Christ means we are willing to go beyond parish boundaries to spread the Good News. How is your parish encouraging this mission orientation?

The Length of the Catechumenate (RCIA, 76)

The RCIA tells us that "the catechumenate is an extended period of time during which the candidates are given suitable pastoral formation and guidance, aimed at training them in the Christian life" (75). A careful reading of the pastoral notes found in the RCIA leads us to understand that the formation of Christians takes a significant amount of time because we are not just expected to instruct candidates in the teaching of the Church, but to form them in the spirit of the Gospel accounts, the practice of charity and mercy, a profound sense of the mystery of Christ, a solidarity with the Christian community, and a commitment to missionary discipleship. With this wider view of Christian formation, it would be unwise to think that we can reduce the initiation of Christians to a series of classroom lessons that have to fit in a typical school year calendar. After many years of pastoral experience it has become ever more evident that a lengthier period for the catechumenate is beneficial. When the RCIA was first implemented, the bishops of the United States already sensed that more time must be allotted to the initiation process than what a school model

During the Period of the Catechumenate, catechumens are formed in the spirit of the Gospel accounts.

(fall to spring) allows. Consequently, the National Conference of Catholic Bishops (now the United States Conference of Catholic Bishops) issued the *National Statutes for the Catechumenate*. The statutes regarding the catechumenate in the United States direct that the catechumenate period "should extend at least one year of formation, instruction, and probation. Ordinarily this period should go from at least the Easter season of one year until the next; preferably it should begin before Lent in one year and extend until Easter of the following year" (*National Statutes for the Catechumenate*, 6). Since the *National Statutes for the Catechumenate* was issued in 1986, pastoral ministers responsible for the RCIA in parishes have not only recognized the wisdom behind the document, but have also begun to suggest that a still much longer period for the catechumenate may be advisable.

The length of the catechumenate, of course, depends on the needs of the catechumens. It would be best not to begin our initiation ministry with a predetermined number of months required. The natural inclination in North America is to follow a school-year calendar and force the catechumenate period into a short time frame, from late autumn to spring. We certainly want to designate Easter as the primary time for celebrating the sacraments of initiation. But telescoping the catechumenate into a period between late fall and Ash Wednesday creates an unhealthy time crunch that ordinarily does not allow sufficient time for faith to mature.

Baptized candidates preparing for reception into full communion may or may not need as extensive a catechumenate period as catechumens. The length of the period for candidates depends entirely on their background, level of faith, commitment to Christ and his Church, and integration of the Church's teaching.

Parishes are gradually finding that an ongoing catechumenate is most effective. Using the liturgical year and the Lectionary as the guide, source, and pathway more readily facilitates an ongoing catechumenate. In this way, individual catechumens and candidates can enter and leave this period at any time depending on their own spiritual condition and readiness to move forward. What this presumes is that when people first express interest in pursuing initiation, we will not give them a set calendar that predetermines the dates when they will enter the catechumenate and celebrate the initiation sacraments. From our very first encounters with inquirers, we need to set out the implications that conversion, formation, mission readiness, and sacramental participation require of every mature Christian. What we have to help inquirers to understand is that initiation is not academic coursework to be completed, but a way of life to be developed.

———— ◆ ————

Questions for Discussion and Reflection

1. How long generally is your parish catechumenate process? What steps can you take to extend this period and keep it open ended so someone can enter the catechumenate at any time?

2. Think about three major feasts. What basic Catholic teachings emerge from these feasts?

3. Are catechumens and candidates always included in the same sessions together? What distinction do you provide given the difference in their baptismal status?

———— ◆ ————

They have tried to live as God's
faithful followers.

The Second Step: Rite of Election or Enrollment of Names

The Period of the Catechumenate ends with the Rite of Election or Enrollment of Names on or near the First Sunday of Lent (see RCIA, 129–137). In this rite, the Church states her intention to baptize the catechumens at Easter. The rite presumes that the Church is certain of several things: that the catechumens' conversion has matured, that their minds and morals are Christ-like, and that the practice of faith and charity is evident in their daily lives. These catechumens are not expected to be perfect, but it must be evident that the way of Jesus is becoming their way of life even while they must still deal with their own faults, hesitations, and sinfulness.[17]

> Before the Rite of Election is celebrated, the catechumens are expected to have undergone a conversion in mind and in action and to have developed a sufficient acquaintance with Christian teaching as well as a spirit of faith and charity. With deliberate will and an enlightened faith they must have the intention to receive the sacraments of the church, a resolve they will express publicly in the actual celebration of the rite.[18]

The questions asked of godparents during the rite give some indication of what is expected before the catechumens are chosen for the initiation sacraments. The bishop inquires:

- Have they faithfully listened to the word of God proclaimed by the Church?
- Have they responded to that word and begun to walk in God's presence?
- Have they shared the company of their Christian brothers and sisters and joined with them in prayer?[19]

---

17. An outline of the rite is found on page 93. Proper texts "For the Election or Enrollment of Names" are found in the third edition of *The Roman Missal*. These texts are used if, "for pastoral reasons, [the Rite of Election] is celebrated apart from [the First Sunday of Lent]." The Mass of the Friday of the Fourth Week of Lent may also be used if the Rite of Election takes place at a time other than the First Sunday of Lent.
18. RCIA, 120.
19. RCIA, 131.

AN INTRODUCTION TO THE RCIA

These questions summarize the dialogue that is to take place between catechumens and their catechumenal communities long before the celebration of the rite. Before the invitation to celebrate the Rite of Election is extended, the catechumen meets with one or more members of the catechumenate team to discuss the catechumen's readiness. The task of the Church at this time—carried out by the bishop, pastor, catechist, and sponsors—is to discern in the catechumens a genuine response to the call to Christian discipleship.

Catechumenal ministers must take this discernment process seriously. While the idea of choosing people for initiation may seem to some, especially those who place a high value on privacy and individualism, to be elitist, the Church would be remiss in initiating an individual for whom the catechumenal process has made no difference in their life or who is not yet ready to participate fully in the Church's life. When it appears that an individual's disposition or motives for initiation are not clear to us or to the individual, we have a responsibility to question that person's readiness.

Initiation ministers should dialogue with catechumens about their spiritual growth and readiness throughout the process.

This discernment is not a judgment made hastily or by surprise. There ought to be dialogue throughout the process, which naturally comes to a point of decision prior to the celebration of the Rite of Election.

Just as we can take the discernment process too lightly, so can we become too idealistic or unreasonable in our expectations of catechumens. We are not making a judgment on their sanctity but on their readiness for the Christian life. Catechumenal ministers will find the discernment process challenging to their own faith. Their awareness of their own need for growth should help them be more realistic in their expectations of the catechumens.

The bishop ordinarily presides over the Rite of Election. As pastor of the diocesan Church, the bishop formally chooses, or "elects," men and women for the celebration of the sacraments of initiation at the Easter Vigil. This election is reminiscent of Israel's election by God to be a people of the covenant. The Rite of Election carries with it the echo of Jesus' words, "It was not you who chose me, but I who chose you" (John 15:16). As the names of the catechumens are called and inscribed in the Book of the Elect, catechumens and assembly are reminded that these catechumens are known by God and personally called by name. While we play our part as catechumenal ministers by planting the seeds for conversion, ultimately it is God who gives the growth.

When the bishop presides over a diocesan celebration of the Rite of Election at the cathedral church or in the regions of the diocese, it becomes clear that the catechumens are being chosen for initiation into a Church that extends beyond the parish communities from which they come. They are being called to live in communion with the universal Church, for which they must also show their concern and solidarity.

When the bishop presides over a diocesan Rite of Election, this clarifies to the catechumens that they are being initiated into a universal Church.

In preparation for the Rite of Election a parish may wish to celebrate a Rite of Sending the Catechumens for Election (see RCIA, 106–117). This rite allows the local community to hear the testimony of sponsors and catechists on behalf of the catechumens and to support them with their prayers. The catechumens are sent to the Rite of Election knowing that the prayers and affirmation of their community are behind them.

---◆---

Questions for Discussion and Reflection

1. What question would you personally like to ask catechumens to discern their readiness for the initiation sacraments?

2. Try to imagine yourself in the shoes of a catechumen at the Rite of Election. What do you suppose you would learn from the experience?

---◆---

Rite of Calling the Candidates to Continuing Conversion

The edition of the RCIA approved for use in the United States provides a celebration for baptized candidates that is inspired by the Rite of Election.[20] Because they are already baptized, candidates who are completing their initiation through the Sacraments of Confirmation and Eucharist, and candidates for reception into the full communion of the Catholic Church are already God's elect. Unlike the Rite of Election for catechumens, this rite does not call candidates to Baptism, but rather invites them into an intensive period of spiritual preparation for the Sacraments of Confirmation and Eucharist. The desire of baptized candidates to deepen their faith and strengthen their membership in the Church can be ritually acknowledged in the Rite of Calling the Candidates to Continuing Conversion (see RCIA, 446–458). This rite may be celebrated in the parish or it may be the custom in some dioceses to do a combined rite with the diocesan celebration of the Rite of Election (see RCIA, 547–561). Because our ministry to baptized candidates may be within a much shorter period of time, it is conceivable that this optional rite adapted for those who are being received into full communion could be celebrated in the parish more than one time during the year. It is also possible that this adapted rite might be celebrated at a smaller gathering of the faithful, such as at a daily Mass.

The questions that the celebrant asks the sponsors in this adapted rite for baptized candidates indicate what ministry calls for prior to celebrating this rite and outlines the criteria we can use to discern the readiness of candidates for the sacraments:

- "Have they faithfully listened to the apostles' instruction proclaimed by the Church?"
- "Have they come to a deeper appreciation of their baptism, in which they were joined to Christ and his Church?"

---

20. An outline of the rite is found on page 94.

When combined rites—those that include both catechumens and candidates—are celebrated, every effort must be made to avoid any confusion that would blur the distinction between the baptized and the unbaptized.

- "Have they reflected sufficiently on the tradition of the Church, which is their heritage, and joined their brothers and sisters in prayer?"[21]

When combined rites—those that include both catechumens and candidates—are celebrated, every effort must be made to avoid any confusion that would blur the distinction between the baptized and the unbaptized. Failing to make that distinction weakens the appreciation of the dignity of Christian Baptism and is ecumenically offensive. The Sacrament of Baptism marks a radical change in an individual. St. Paul uses the imagery of death and coming to life to convey what occurs in the waters of Baptism:

> Are you unaware that we who were baptized into Christ Jesus were baptized into his death? We were indeed buried with him through baptism into death, so that, just as Christ was raised from the dead by the glory of the Father, we too might live in newness of life.[22]

When we do anything that appears to overlook or dismiss the one-time-only nature of Baptism, we are diminishing the dramatic effect of Baptism which irrevocably claims us for Christ. Christian Baptisms even outside the Roman Catholic tradition are generally accepted as valid and should be respected as a sacrament in which all Christians have a common origin.

---

21. RCIA, 453.
22. Romans 6:3–4.

The Period of Purification and Enlightenment

The third period of the initiation process is the Period of Purification and Enlightenment. This period begins with the celebration of the Rite of Election. The period coincides with Lent, a season of penance and conversion leading to Baptism or baptismal renewal at Easter. During this time, the catechumens reflect on their faith and religious experience in a more intense manner. They take all that they have heard and seen, learned, prayed and shared, and they ponder it all in the depths of their hearts. Lent supports this process of interiorizing, giving it shape and direction through the Scriptures, prayers, and traditional Lenten disciplines of fasting, performing works of mercy, charity, and penance, and being committed to personal sacrifice (prayer, fasting, and almsgiving).

Examination of Life

From Ash Wednesday to Holy Thursday, the entire Church community reexamines its life. Lent is a time to cleanse ourselves of what may stand in the way of living for the Kingdom of God. Lent enlightens and uncovers the truth—the true way of life, the true path to holiness, the Kingdom of God to which we are called.

Several traditional elements help us achieve these Lenten ideals. Being mindful of the food we eat by fasting and abstaining involves the whole person. Works of charity and almsgiving remedy the self-centered mind-set that can so easily entrap us. Penitential acts and prayers are humble admissions that we have sinned.

Lent is not so much a time for catechesis as it is a retreat preparing us for the initiation sacraments of Easter. This period finds its direction in the liturgy. The *Lectionary for Mass* and *The Roman Missal* are our guides for the Lenten Period of Purification and Enlightenment.[23]

The parish's Lenten discipline will affect the lives of the elect (the title now given to the catechumens who will be initiated at the coming Easter) and candidates, and in turn the elect and candidates can have a powerful

---

23. See also below regarding the scrutinies and exorcisms that take place during Lent.

effect on the assembly. The elect and candidates are themselves the primary symbol for Lent. We see in them what we ought to see happening in ourselves: a conversion that leaves us with a hunger for Eucharist and a thirst for building God's Kingdom.

Scrutinies and Exorcisms

The gift of conversion is strengthened and deepened through the scrutinies and exorcisms, which take place on the Third, Fourth, and Fifth Sundays of Lent (see RCIA, 141–156, 164–170, and 171–177). "Scrutiny" may seem an odd word to use in this situation, but it describes well what happens when the Word of God is proclaimed.[24] God's Word searches our hearts and scrutinizes our values and way of life. This scrutinizing begins outside the formal rites—throughout Lent and long before—as the elect search their lives in the light of the Gospel and so identify the falsehoods that keeps them from embracing the Kingdom of God as their way of life.

When the evils, temptations, and falsehoods from which we need to be freed have been identified through such scrutiny, there is need for exorcism. These evils are forceful obstacles to our living for the Kingdom of God. They include some of the most powerful forces of our age: materialism, consumerism, sexism, racism, militarism, hedonism, and idolatry in many forms. There are also personal weaknesses that can be obstacles to our spiritual growth such as long standing grudges, selfishness, poor health habits, personal prejudices, addictions to social media, and so forth. We all recognize the falsehoods we encounter every day in advertising, media, pleasure-seeking ideology, moral relativism, and so on which promise us immediate gratification but not necessarily happiness and long term satisfaction. These are the cultural demons that can destroy our lives if we let them.

The exorcism prayers in the RCIA are somewhat generic. They speak of falsehood, blindness, evil, the "father of lies." For these words to have meaning, the elect must be helped to name the falsehood and blindness that we are subjected to. These exorcism prayers also tell us what ought to be happening in Lent for all the members of the Church: renunciation of the demons of falsehood that charade as god. Exorcisms are not primarily rites of forgiveness or reconciliation, but of liberation. The scrutinies and exorcisms aim to remove whatever obstacles may still remain before

---

24. An outline of the three scrutiny rites are found on page 94. The Mass texts, "For the Celebration of the Scrutinies," are found in the Ritual Masses section of the third edition of *The Roman Missal*. Proper texts are provided for the First, Second, and Third Scrutiny.

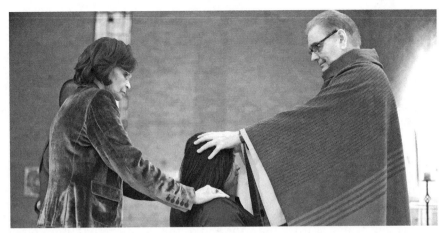

The scrutinies and exorcisms aim to remove whatever obstacles still remain for the catechumens before they are initiated.

celebrating the sacraments of initiation, freed of the temptation to walk away from Baptism. During the celebration of the scrutiny, the elect and the baptized members of the community may recognize that they have given in to evils that have blinded them. For this the exorcism prayers ask forgiveness, which the elect will receive through Baptism. For all of us who are baptized, the Sacrament of Penance will be our cleansing of sin.

The exorcism prayers of the scrutinies were composed for catechumens, thus the imagery in the prayers refers to the preparation for Baptism. The RCIA reserves the the scrutinies and exorcisms on the Third, Fourth, and Fifth Sundays of Lent for the unbaptized (see RCIA, 463).

Penitential Rite

Baptized candidates for reception into full communion with the Church do not participate in the scrutinies and exorcisms with the elect because they have already been claimed by Christ for God in Baptism. They can be confident that the grace of their Baptism and their identity in Christ gives them the strength to combat evil. However, the United States edition of the RCIA includes a Penitential Rite that is designed in the spirit of a scrutiny for baptized candidates (see RCIA, 459–472). This rite may be celebrated on the Second Sunday of Lent or on a Lenten weekday.[25] This Penitential Rite helps to prepare the candidates for the celebration of the Sacrament of Penance and may be used in preparation for reception into full communion of the Catholic Church at any time of the year. The

---

25. An outline of the rite is found on page 94.

National Statutes for the Catechumenate regulating the practice of Christian initiation in the United States encourage the celebration of the Sacrament of Penance prior to and distinct from the celebration of the Rite of Reception into the Full Communion of the Catholic Church (see 36).

Preparatory Rites on Holy Saturday

Those who are to be initiated at the Easter Vigil are encouraged to gather for prayer during the day of Holy Saturday. Catechumens who have now been elected for Baptism and candidates who will be received into full communion of the Catholic Church, along with the entire community, are instructed to keep the Vigil and extend the Paschal fast of Good Friday throughout Holy Saturday until the end of the evening Vigil liturgy (see *National Statutes for the Catechumenate*, 15, and canon 1251 from the *Code of Canon Law*). This is not a penitential fast but a fast of joy and anticipation of the sacred mysteries.

Several rites are recommended for use on Holy Saturday during the day, although not all of these rites would necessarily be used. Local needs and diocesan directives may prescribe which are the most appropriate to celebrate and how.

Rites that may be used include the Recitation of the Creed (see RCIA, 193–196), Ephphetha Rite (see RCIA, 197–199), and Choosing a Baptismal Name (see RCIA, 200–205). An anointing with the oil of catechumens (see RCIA, 98–103) may also be used for the unbaptized, if pastorally appropriate. A model for a celebration of the preparation rites is offered (see RCIA, 187–192).

———— ◆ ————

Questions for Discussion and Reflection

1. How does the spirit and discipline of Lent give the Period of Purification and Enlightenment its shape and tone?

2. How might the community's Lenten discipline influence the elect's experience of the Period of Purification and Enlightenment?

3. What are some of the evils, temptations, and falsehoods that need to be exorcized from today's world?

———— ◆ ————

The Third Step: The Celebration of the Sacraments of Christian Initiation

Baptism

The focus of the Easter Vigil is on Jesus Christ dead and risen. It is not a "graduation" or testimonial for those who are being baptized. The candidates for Baptism and reception into the Church show us, in their transformation this night, that Christ has indeed been raised. He has given us new life through his victory over sin and death. In his dying and rising we see more clearly the shape of our own lives.[26]

The Liturgy of Baptism takes place after the homily. The elect who have been prepared for Baptism are called by name and come forward with their godparents. As the Litany of Saints is chanted, the deacon takes the Paschal candle and leads the catechumens to the font.

After a solemn blessing of the baptismal water, the priest celebrant invites the candidates for Baptism to renounce all evil and to profess their faith in the Father, the Son, and the Holy Spirit. The whole process of the catechumenate reaches a climax as the elect publicly profess the faith they will live for the rest of their lives.

Baptism follows immediately. Immersion is the preferred way of baptizing. *Christian Initiation,* General Introduction states, "Either immersion, which is more suitable as a symbol of participation in the death and resurrection of Christ, or pouring may lawfully be used" (22) in the celebration of Baptism.

The *National Statutes for the Catechumenate* states:

> Baptism by immersion is the fuller and more expressive sign of the sacrament and, therefore . . . provision should be made for its more frequent use in the baptism of adults.[27]

The newly baptized are clothed in a baptismal robe or gown. Godparents may assist in the vesting. When Baptism is by partial or total

---

26. An outline of the celebration of the sacraments of Christian initiation is found on page 95.
27. *National Statutes for the Catechumenate*, 17.

immersion, the newly baptized may be led to adjacent rooms where they dress in their baptismal robes before returning to the assembly. They are then presented with a candle lit from the Paschal candle.[28]

———— • • ————

Questions for Discussion and Reflection

1. How is Baptism at the Easter Vigil another way we proclaim the Easter Gospel?

2. What do you remember about past experiences of Christian initiation at the Easter Vigil?

3. What are the pros and cons of including the baptized candidates in the initiation rites at the Easter Vigil?

———— • • ————

Renewal of Baptismal Promises and Reception into Full Communion

The celebrant then invites the community to a solemn renewal of baptismal promises. The congregation publicly renounces sin and rejects Satan. They are asked to confess their belief in Father, Son, and Holy Spirit. These are the vows upon which our Christian discipleship rests and upon which our unity and identity as the Body of Christ, the Church, is built. If there are candidates for Reception into Full Communion, they join the community in the renewal of baptismal vows. The celebrant continues with the Rite of Reception into the Full Communion with the Catholic Church. The celebrant formally welcomes them into full communion (see RCIA, 586 and RCIA, 473–504) saying:

> N., the Lord receives you into the Catholic Church.
> His loving kindness had led you here,
> so that in the unity of the Holy Spirit
> you may have full communion with us
> in the faith that you have professed in the presence of his family.[29]

After a sprinkling with the baptismal water, those who have professed their faith and have been received into the full communion of the Church

---

28. When preparing the Vigil liturgy and the initiation rites, parish ministers should consult the texts for the Easter Vigil from the third edition of *The Roman Missal* in addition to the *Rite of Christian Initiation of Adults.*

29. RCIA, 492.

await the newly baptized, who had exited to change clothes. Then the newly baptized, those received into full communion, and those Catholics completing their Christian initiation, are now confirmed (see RCIA, 587–591).[30] The celebration of Reception into Full Communion may take place at times other times in the year other than the Easter Vigil. Candidates for Reception into Full Communion do not always need an extensive period of catechesis, especially when they might have been active in the parish for years although never formally received into the Church. They can be received into the Church when they are ready. They do not have to wait for months when it is not necessary.

Confirmation

The RCIA, *National Statutes for the Catechumenate*, and the *Code of Canon Law*, 883 §2, stress the importance of celebrating Confirmation immediately after Baptism so that, with the Eucharist, these sacraments will be understood as one integral action of Christ initiating new members into his Church.

In accord with the ancient practice followed in the Roman liturgy, adults are not to be baptized without receiving confirmation immediately afterward, unless some serious reason stands in the way. The conjunction of the two celebrations signifies the unity of the paschal mystery, the close link between the mission of the Son and the outpouring of the Holy Spirit, and the connection of the two sacraments through which the Son and the Holy Spirit come with the Father to those who are baptized.[31]

The Sacraments of Baptism, Confirmation, and Eucharist are the one action of Christ initiating new members into his Church.

In order to signify clearly the interrelation or coalescence of the three sacraments which are required for full Christian initiation (canon 842:2), adult candidates,

---

30. Note that the Confirmation of those who are already Catholic only takes place if the priest has received permission from the local bishop.

31. RCIA, 215.

Participating in the Eucharist means the neophytes may now give God thanks and offer him their very selves.

> including children of catechetical age, are to receive baptism, confirmation, and eucharist in a single eucharistic celebration, whether at the Easter Vigil or, if necessary, at some other time.[32]

It should be noted that the above directive on Confirmation applies to all children of catechetical age. The priest who baptizes an individual of catechetical age or receves them into full communion of the Catholic Church automatically has the right to confirm that person within the same ritual celebration. The priest does not need special permission to do so. In fact, he is required by law to confirm.

First Sharing in the Celebration of the Eucharist

After the newly initiated are sealed with the gift of the Holy Spirit, they are led to the Eucharistic table. "With the entire community they share in the offering of the sacrifice and say the Lord's Prayer, giving expression to the spirit of adoption as God's children" (RCIA, 217). Now sharing in the royal priesthood of Christ, the neophytes (as the newly baptized are called) may participate in the Universal Prayer (or Prayer of the Faithful) and be invited to bring the gifts of bread and wine to the altar. Participating in the Universal Payer at Mass is not just a charitable thing to do, it is now part of the newly baptized person's "job description," namely to intercede for the needs of the world and the Church before God.

---

32. *National Statutes for the Catechumenate*, 14.

Participation in the Eucharist means that the neophytes now have both the right and the responsibility to "give thanks to God and offer the unblemished sacrificial Victim not only by the means of the hands of the Priest but also together with him and so that they may learn to offer their very selves" (*General Instruction of the Roman Missal*, 95). Together with the whole Church they enter ever more deeply into the dying and rising of the Lord, whose flesh and blood seals their participation in the new covenant. The Eucharist is the repeatable sacrament of initiation, which draws the baptized with every Eucharist into the heart of the Paschal Mystery. Every celebration of the Eucharist, then, is an opportunity to renew what was begun in Baptism and Confirmation. At the same time, the Eucharist becomes the bridge that extends into the world, where the baptized must learn to be bread broken and wine poured out for their sisters and brothers. Speaking in Santa Cruz, Bolivia, Pope Francis said: "The Eucharist is a missionary sacrament; it calls people to give all they are and have to God, seek his blessing and then take his love to the world."[33]

Questions for Discussion and Reflection

1. How would you describe the Eucharist as the culmination of the initiation process but also the repeatable sacrament of initiation?

2. What is the practice in your parish initiating children of catechetical age with the celebration of Baptism, Confirmation, and Eucharist in the same liturgy?

3. How are the elect and candidates taught to fully participate in the Mass by joining their lives and their sacrifices with Christ's?

---

33. From his homily in Santa Cruz, Bolivia, July 9, 2015. Quoted in Cindy Wooden, "Eucharistic sharing is call to mission, to feeding the poor, pope says in Bolivia," Catholic News Service, *Catholic Standard*, July 10, 2015, http://catholicstandard.org/Content/Social/Social/Article /Eucharistic-sharing-is-call-to-mission-to-feeding-the-poor-pope-says-in-Bolivia/-2/-2/6723.

Period of Postbaptismal Catechesis or Mystagogy

The final period in the initiation process is postbaptismal catechesis, or *mystagogy* (which means "teaching the mysteries"). We might be inclined to consider the initiation process completed with the Easter Vigil, but the order of initiation provides yet another moment in the whole process: a time for neophytes to adjust to their vocation within the Church and to deepen their understanding of the Paschal Mystery by drawing from their experience of the community and the sacraments (see RCIA, 244–251 and *National Statutes for the Catechumenate*, 22–24).

This postbaptismal period can be difficult for the newly received members of the Church. The rites of the catechumenate and the Vigil are past, primary catechesis is completed, and the catechumenal community, which at one time formed such a closely knit group, and was so involved with the candidates, is now expanded to include the entire baptized community. Not only do they need to know that the community is still interested in them, but they need to find their place in its ordinary daily life. There is an adjustment to be made, but the pride of belonging to the Christian community and the support that comes with being one with all the baptized should gradually become a source of comfort, support, and motivation for mission.

The newly initiated, fresh in their experience of the Easter sacraments, are ripe for a deeper journey into the sacramental dimension of life. Now they can talk about the sacraments not as something they are anticipating, but as something they have personally experienced. This is what we mean by *mystagogy*. The most appropriate place for mystagogical catechesis is at Sunday Mass (Eucharist). The Scriptures and prayers of Easter Time are a gradual unfolding of the meaning and implications of the Sacraments of Baptism, Confirmation, and Eucharist. The homilist can draw from the richness of the biblical Easter narratives, the Acts of the Apostles, the Easter symbols, and sacramental celebrations that are still fresh in the memory of the newly initiated and the congregation.

Many find this period of the initiation process the most difficult to implement in the parish. Our contemporary culture seems to be losing the art of contemplation that moves us to reflect upon our experiences to draw out deeper meanings and truths. This contemplative review of what we have heard and experienced can be taught earlier in the initiation process. Now in Easter Time when we are immersed in the celebration of the Risen Christ, there should be much to explore.

During the Period of Mystagogy, neophytes may be provided opportunities for praying and sharing insights in a less formal setting.

Parish ministers must be patient in developing this post-baptismal period. In addition to the celebration of Sunday Eucharist, opportunities for sharing and praying in less structured settings may be helpful. Some have found that sharing insights and memories of the catechumenate and Easter Vigil happens naturally at a festive meal or a party during Easter Time.

In developing an effective mystagogy we need to look for mystagogues —individuals who have a special gift for uncovering what we know by experience or believe in the heart. The early Fathers of the Church were great mystagogues. Reading some of the homilies and letters of Cyril of Jerusalem, Ambrose of Milan, or Theodore of Mopsuestia will provide insight into the deeper levels of the meaning and experience of sacramental life. Readings found in the *Liturgy of the Hours* during Easter Time provide easy access to these masterpieces of mystagogia. What is characteristic in the writings of these mystagogues is their poetry and their careful attention to symbol. This is not a time for the kind of theological analysis one might expect in a classroom. Rather, it is a time to explore at a different level the deeply human and spiritual experiences of those whose lives have been touched profoundly in the sacraments of initiation.

The Period of Mystagogy will be most effective in communities where the Fifty Days of Easter are celebrated well. Easter Time becomes the environment in which mystagogy takes place. These Fifty Days ought to be filled with festivity and beauty, parties, and special celebrations. The music, art and decoration, preaching, and liturgies of Easter Time are all important for giving mystagogy its proper framework. It may also be an opportune time to invite the neophytes to offer a brief testimony at one of the Sunday Masses during the Fifty Days of Easter.

Easter Time is also an appropriate time for the bishop to celebrate the Eucharist with the newly initiated of the diocese. This is an occasion for the diocesan Church to give thanks to God for the life that the newly initiated bring to the Church. At this celebration the bishop may congratulate and joyfully welcome the newly initiated into the Eucharistic community. Like the Rite of Election, this is an opportunity for the bishop to establish a pastoral relationship with the newly initiated and to point to the universal nature of the Church united under a common shepherd. The bishop may want to take this occasion to personally charge the newly initiated to be missionary disciples who share their joy with others as Mary Magdalene did with the Apostles on Easter morning.

The bishops of the United States have determined that the period of mystagogy should extend for a full year, until the anniversary of initiation (see *National Statutes for the Catechumenate*, 24). The bishops have suggested that it may be helpful to assemble the newly initiated at least monthly for ongoing formation and pastoral care.

Easter Time is also an appropriate time for the bishop to celebrate the Eucharist with and congratulate and welcome the newly initiated of the diocese.

Because each new Catholic's needs are different from another's needs, there is a caution about establishing too formal or rigid a structure for mystagogy. The key is pastoral care. The parish staff, the catechumenate team, and especially godparents will perform an important ministry by keeping contact with the newly initiated. Through sensitive pastoral care we can discover what the newly initiated need, lead them into closer communion with the Church, foster a deeper exploration of the mysteries, and support a wholesome and integrated Catholic Christian lifestyle.[34]

---

34. For a detailed pastoral study on the implementation of the various rites of Christian initiation, consult *Guide for Celebrating® Christian Initiation with Adults* by Victoria M. Tufano, Paul Turner, and D. Todd Williamson and published by Liturgy Training Publications, as well as *Guide for Celebrating® Christian Initiation with Children* by Rita Burns Senseman, Victoria M. Tufano, Paul Turner, and D. Todd Williamson also published by Liturgy Training Publications.

CHAPTER FOUR

THE CALL TO SERVE INCLUDES ALL THE BAPTIZED

Becoming a mature adult involves others in your life. You may have heard the old cliché that "it takes a village to raise a child." The formation and initiation of a Christian also requires a "village" to raise up a man or woman who desires to be a faithful disciple of Jesus. You can interpret "village" to mean the Christian community, your parish. The RCIA tells us:

> The people of God, as represented by the local Church, should understand and show by their concern that the initiation of adults is the responsibility of all the baptized. Therefore the community must always be fully prepared in the pursuit of its apostolic vocation to give help to those who are searching for Christ.[1]

The faithful play an important role when they take catechumens and candidates into their circles to openly discuss faith and the Christian life, praying with them and for them, giving honest and prudent testimony about them, and actively participating in the liturgical celebrations of the initiation process. A community's hospitality and its witness to Gospel values will greatly help catechumens and candidates become active participants in the Church's life and mission. If the catechumens and candidates feel welcomed only by a handful of parishioners, their integration into the Christian community will be incomplete. They should sense the interest and charity of the whole congregation because it is into the whole community, not just into the RCIA group, that catechumens and candidates are being initiated.

---

1. RCIA, 9.

Many Catholics, unfortunately, do not see that they have any responsibility for initiating new members. Some Catholics view faith as something very private and do not appreciate the importance of community. They may feel that initiating new members is the pastor's responsibility shared with a small number of volunteers. Perhaps some Catholics feel like no one ever welcomed them into the Church or the parish, so they wonder why they need to reach out to those who want to become Catholic. Some parishioners may feel that they aren't competent to be a catechist or sponsor. The formation of communities that understand and appreciate the meaning of their own Baptism and the value of a supportive community of faith is an ongoing pastoral concern. A parish whose parishioners appreciate their baptismal identity and exercise their baptismal vocation in prayer, community life, Gospel witness, charity, and mission becomes the ideal setting for the catechumenate. Faith is not found in a book but in the lives of believing Christians. Consequently it is of utmost

A parish whose parishioners and staff appreciate their baptismal identity and exercise their baptismal vocation is the ideal setting for the catechumenate.

importance that candidates and catechumens learn the faith of the Church from those who profess the faith and witness to the faith in the ordinary circumstances in life.

Ministries

The long and yet incomplete list of ministries noted in this resource may leave one with the impression that initiation is a very complex network of ministries and sophisticated structures. This need not be so.

In smaller parishes, especially in rural areas, there may be frustration because the number of those available to minister on a catechumenate team may be few. But smaller parishes often have the advantage of being close-knit communities where the parish itself is truly the catechumenal community. The mark of an effective catechumenate is not the number of different ministries that can be created or how intricate or how complex preparations can be developed. Rather, the ultimate test is whether the inquirers, catechumens, candidates, elect, and newly initiated are experiencing a genuine welcome and are absorbing the Catholic way of life.

Large city and suburban parishes often must develop complex structures because of a great number of catechumens and candidates. Rural communities and smaller city parishes need not try to model their pastoral plan on the large-parish paradigm. Smaller communities have strengths upon which they should build their own structure and network of ministries. University campuses will likewise need to develop their own schedule and style for a suitable catechumenate. In some areas, several parishes may share one pastor and a number of other ministries. In these situations, some elements of the catechumenal process can be shared together. Ordinarily, the rites of initiation would be celebrated in the candidate's or catechumen's parish. The local parish is entrusted in a special way with initiating those who will become fellow parishioners. The local parish will become their spiritual home and is the most appropriate place for their initiation.

While the whole believing community takes responsibility for forming those who will be initiated, a few designated members are asked to assume additional responsibilities for the care of catechumens and candidates. These designated ministers include sponsors, godparents, catechists, spiritual advisors, mentors for mission, and a catechumenate director. Priests and deacons, of course, form part of the team that will surround the candidates and catechumens on their path to the initiation sacraments, but they ought not be the only individuals who minister, inspire, shape, and catechize. These different ministers should not operate as "specialized experts" who come into the formation circle, perform their expertise, and leave. Rather, all who are engaged in forming candidates and catechumens will hopefully understand themselves to be one pastoral team ministering collaboratively.

Sponsors

The RCIA describes sponsors as "persons who have known and assisted the candidates and stand as witnesses to the candidates' moral character, faith, and intention" (10). Later the RCIA adds:

> Helped by the example and support of sponsors, godparents, and the entire Christian community, the catechumens learn to turn more readily to God in prayer, to bear witness to the faith, in all things to keep their

hopes set on Christ, to follow supernatural inspiration in their deeds, and to practice love of neighbor, even at the cost of self-renunciation.[2]

Through the sponsor, the catechumen or candidate will experience most directly the spirit and belief of the community. The sponsor ordinarily will be the one who introduces the catechumen or candidate to other members of the community and its various ministries and activities.

The RCIA does not indicate whether a catechumen or candidate can have more than one sponsor, but there does not seem to be any reason why this could not be allowed. On occasion, a catechumen or candidate may desire to choose a relative or close friend as their sponsor. However, the family member or friend may not be familiar with the parish into which the catechumen or candidate is being initiated. In this case, a parish may designate someone else to act as sponsor. The value of a parish-designated sponsor is that this sponsor will be very familiar with parish life and Catholic teaching and culture in general. Most often, however, a catechumen or candidate will depend on one adult, someone he or she can trust and feel comfortable with, whether that is a family member or a parishioner.

Spouses ordinarily are not recommended as sponsors. While most candidates will naturally share questions and insights with their spouses, there is a value in a candidate having someone outside the marriage with whom to share questions and even apprehensions on their spiritual journey. Spouses should, however, be invited to participate in the initiation process so that husbands and wives can grow together through the experience.

Sponsors should be faithful Catholics who are comfortable relating with others and are secure in their faith. They should have a balanced spirituality and a love for the Church and be free of any personal agendas that would jeopardize the process. Sponsors ordinarily are chosen from the parish by the catechumenate team, working in close collaboration with the pastoral staff. A sponsor should assume sponsorship for one individual for as long as that might take. The practice of keeping a permanent pool of parish sponsors who are called upon each year is not to be encouraged. We need to keep a larger-community focus and encourage others to become involved in the process.

The sponsor's responsibilities include: keeping in regular contact with the catechumens and candidates, encouraging them, listening to their

---

2. RCIA, 75 §2.

Godparents are to show catechumens how to live a Gospel-centered life.

questions and their doubts, sharing time and experience in a friendly manner, participating in catechumenate sessions, praying with and for those they sponsor, and introducing them to the other members of the community. Potential sponsors may participate in the inquiry period even if they are not assigned to a particular candidate until some months later.

The sponsor's role continues until the Rite of Election, when godparents begin to accompany the elect and the candidates to the Easter sacraments. Sponsors do, however, continue to participate in the catechumenal community in support of the elect and the candidates. A sponsor may also serve as godparent to the one he or she has sponsored.

Godparents

The ministry of the godparent is similar to that of the sponsor.

> Godparents are persons chosen by the candidates on the basis of example, good qualities, and friendship, delegated by the local Christian community, and approved by the priest. It is the responsibility of godparents to show the candidates how to practice the Gospel in personal and social life, to sustain the candidates in moments of hesitancy and anxiety, to bear witness, and to guide the candidates' progress in the baptismal life.[3]

The godparent is similar to the sponsor in that he or she is expected to be a person of faith, to profess and live by Christian values, and to be capable of communicating faith and values to the elect.

Godparents assume their ministry at the Rite of Election and continue to fulfill that role for life. For this reason the godparent should be carefully selected. Although adults usually only have one godparent, there may be two, as with a child. If there is one godparent, it may be either a man or women. If there are two godparents, one must be a male and the other a female, according to the *Code of Canon Law* (see c. 873). Godparents must be mature enough to undertake this responsibility; they must have received

---

3. RCIA, 11.

Because the godparent offers testimony on behalf of the catechumen at the Rite of Election, it is presumed that the godparent already has a relationship with the catechumen.

the three sacraments of initiation: Baptism, Confirmation, and the Eucharist; and they must be members of the Roman Catholic Church free from any impediments or restrictions of Church law that would keep them from carrying out their role. They must also be at least sixteen years old and not be a parent of the one being baptized.

Because the godparent offers testimony on behalf of the catechumen at the Rite of Election, it is presumed that the godparent already has a relationship to the catechumen. If the sponsor becomes the godparent, knowledge of the catechumen can be assured. In many cases a catechumen chooses a friend or family member as godparent. This existing relationship will have to be expanded to include the serious obligations of a godparent to a godchild. This should be clearly explained in one of the catechumenal sessions before the godparents are selected.

Candidates require a sponsor for the Sacrament of Confirmation. In this case, the sponsor's role may begin with the ritual call to continuing conversion, which usually takes place on the First Sunday of Lent. In the event of a Catholic completing his or her Christian initiation, the sponsor for Confirmation may be the godparent from Baptism.

The roles of sponsors and godparents are very similar and the terms are often used interchangeably. The use of the term *godparent* is ordinarily used in reference to the one who accompanies the catechumen to the baptismal font. A godparent's relationship with the baptized is a permanent sacramental relationship defined by canon law. In the case of a person who is preparing for reception into the full communion of the Roman Catholic Church the term *sponsor* is more readily applied. Different ethnic and cultural traditions also may have some bearing on how these roles are interpreted. What is important is that the roles of sponsors and godparents are understood as significant influences in the formation of catechumens and candidates.

Catechumenate Directors

Although it is the pastor's responsibility to oversee the process of Christian initiation and to see that the rites are celebrated with dignity and as intended by the Church's rituals, in many situations it is not practical for the pastor to direct the day-to-day oversight of the catechumenate. He should see to it that someone is appointed for this role who can facilitate the formation process, foster good communication, and organize the efforts of all in the parish.

Catechumenate directors may be members of the parish staff or qualified and trained volunteers. In either case, the director should receive the support and training necessary to exercise his or her role; diocesan pastoral services often are able to provide some assistance and direction. The catechumenate director's responsibilities should be integrated into the larger framework of staff and lay leadership so that the ministry of Christian initiation doesn't become isolated from the rest of parish life. In many dioceses catechumenate directors meet regularly in regions for professional growth and support.

Catechists

Catechists nurture the gift of faith. Respecting the presence of God to each individual, the catechist builds bridges between the experiences of life, the Word of God, and the teaching and prayer of the Church.

The catechist sets the direction and focus for individual catechetical sessions and for the catechetical process as a whole. The catechist must know the traditions and teachings of the Church and appropriate adult learning methods for handing them on. In addition, the catechist must be able to respond to the needs and mentality of a diverse group of catechumens and candidates, who may raise questions and issues that might not have been anticipated. Catechists need to be familiar with the liturgical calendar and the potential of using the liturgical year as the basis for a thorough catechesis. Catechesis that is firmly rooted in the liturgy can be invaluable to candidates and catechumens who learn from this methodology how to draw from the liturgy in the years ahead for further growth in the Christian life. The *National Directory for Catechesis*, the *General Directory for Catechesis*, and the *Catechism of the Catholic Church* are important tools for catechists to use to ensure that connections are made from the Word of God to the official teachings of the Church.

> Catechists should see that their instruction is filled with the spirit of the Gospel, adapted to the liturgical signs and the cycle of the Church's year, suited to the needs of the catechumens, and as far as possible enriched by local traditions.[4]

Catechists represent the Church to those they catechize. Therefore, they must impart the Church's beliefs and not simply their own opinions. Catechists should be well trained for their duties and be people of transparent faith. Those who are well trained in the liturgy and involved in the parish's liturgical life should also be included in the formation of candidates and catechumens. While catechists must be concerned about providing a thorough catechesis, they should keep in mind that the presentation of precepts alone is not sufficient:

> [The catechumenate] is not merely an exposition of dogmatic truths and norms of morality, but a period of formation in the entire Christian life, an apprenticeship of suitable duration, during which the disciples will be joined to Christ their teacher.[5]

Pope Francis has warned against catechesis that is overly doctrinal and yet missing the core message.

> Pastoral ministry in a missionary style is not obsessed with the disjointed transmission of a multitude of doctrines to be insistently imposed. When we adopt a pastoral goal and a missionary style which would actually reach everyone without exception or exclusion, the message has to concentrate on the essentials, on what is most beautiful, most grand, most appealing and at the same time most necessary. The message is simplified, while losing none of its depth and truth, and thus becomes all the more forceful and convincing.[6]

---

4. RCIA, 16.
5. *Ad gentes*, 14.
6. *Evangelii gaudium*, 35.

It is the bishop's responsibility to see that worthy catechists are prepared for this ministry:

> They [bishops] should, furthermore, ensure that catechists are adequately prepared for their task, being well instructed in the doctrine of the church and possessing both a practical and theoretical knowledge of the laws of psychology and of educational method.[7]

Each pastor shares in this duty by ensuring that parish catechists have adequate preparation and continuing formation for their ministry. He should encourage ongoing professional growth. Some of this professional development can be offered through the diocese which might otherwise be difficult for every parish to provide on its own. A grouping of parishes working together with the resources available may also find ways to ensure ongoing professional development and spiritual formation.

Catechists will want to make sure that prayer is an integral part of the plan of catechesis and formation. Catechists will be called on to lead catechumens and candidates in prayer and so should be given the training to do so. At the bishop's discretion, catechists may preside at the minor exorcisms and blessings found in the ritual (see RCIA, 16). Ideally, the parish catechumenate team will involve more than one catechist.

Bishops

As the chief shepherds of the local Church, bishops are the overseers of the Christian initiation process.

> Bishops are the chief stewards of the mysteries of God and leaders of the entire liturgical life in the Church committed to them. This is why they direct the conferring of baptism, which brings to the recipient a share in the kingly priesthood of Christ. Therefore bishops should personally celebrate baptism, especially at the Easter Vigil. They should have a particular concern for the preparation and baptism of adults.[8]

The RCIA gives a more specific description of the bishop's duties regarding the process of initiation:

> The bishop, in person or through his delegate, sets up, regulates, and promotes the program of pastoral formation for catechumens and admits the candidates to their election and to the sacraments. It is hoped that,

---

7. *Christus Dominus*, 14.
8. *Christian Initiation*, General Introduction, 12.

presiding if possible at the Lenten liturgy, he will himself celebrate the rite of election and, at the Easter Vigil, the sacraments of initiation, at least for the initiation of those who are fourteen years old or older. Finally, when pastoral care requires, the bishop should depute catechists, truly worthy and properly prepared, to celebrate the minor exorcisms and the blessings of the catechumens.[9]

The bishop's role in Christian initiation reflects the universal dimension of initiating men and women into the mystery of Christ and his Church. He serves as a bridge between the local parish and the larger Church. His role is not to set up inflexible standards or to develop identical programs for every community but to assure active catechumenates in each area of the diocese and to maintain strong bonds between the catechumens and candidates and the diocesan and universal Church.

In celebrating the Rite of Election at the beginning of Lent, the bishop exercises an important pastoral role (see RCIA, 121). Within the Rite of Election the bishop "declares in the presence of the community the Church's approval of the candidates" (RCIA,122), which is founded on the election by God, in whose name the Church acts (see RCIA, 119). The bishop's involvement in the Rite of Election manifests his role as pastor, teacher, preacher, evangelizer, shepherd, and priest of the local Church.

In preparation for the Rite of Election, the bishop might meet with catechumens and candidates in the course of his pastoral visits throughout the diocese. Listening to their concerns and questions and sharing his own perspective on the Church and its faith can be beneficial to the catechumens and candidates and to the bishop himself. On these visits he might also preside over presentations of the Creed or the Lord's Prayer or one of the scrutinies and exorcisms.

The RCIA notes that the bishop can show his pastoral concern for the new members of the Church by meeting the recently initiated at least once in the year and presiding at the celebration of the Eucharist with them (see RCIA, 251). In some dioceses it has become a custom for the bishop to celebrate a Mass of thanksgiving with the newly initiated during Easter Time.

---

9. RCIA, 12.

Priests

The primary role of the priest in the initiation process is to serve as the overseer of the process in the parish. He sees to it that the vision and process of initiation is woven into the fabric of parish life. He is to take particular care in ministering to the initiation team, offering them support and encouragement, providing for their formation and listening to their needs and experiences.

> Priests, in addition to their usual ministry for any celebration of baptism, confirmation, and the eucharist, have the responsibility of attending to the pastoral and personal care of the catechumens, especially those who seem hesitant and discouraged. With the help of deacons and catechists, they are to provide instruction for the catechumens; they are also to approve the choice of godparents and willingly listen to and help them; they are to be diligent in the correct celebration and adaptation of the rites throughout the whole course of Christian initiation.[10]

While the priest is a steward of God's Word and the Church's teachings, he exercises his responsibility for catechesis with others who have been prepared for this ministry. Not to share this responsibility could result in giving the unfortunate impression to catechumens and candidates that the laity are not capable of communicating the faith or not expected to do so.

One of the most important roles entrusted to the priest is to preside at the various rites of initiation. As the preacher on these occasions, the priest must be well acquainted with the catechumens and candidates. He needs to know something of their backgrounds and of their hopes, fears, and doubts so that he can preach the Word of God effectively to them and to the community that gathers with them.

Although the parish priest should take a great interest in the Church's order of initiation, it would be shortsighted of him to assume total responsibility for the initiation process. The vision of the Church's way of initiating new Catholics demands that lay leaders from the community are an integral and active part of the process. This helps assure that Christian initiation is anchored in parish life and not totally dependent on the ordained pastor as the sole minister of Christian initiation.

---

10. RCIA, 13.

For many priests, convert instructions of the past were a very satisfying part of priestly ministry. The individual, personal contact with adults over matters of spiritual depth and meaning left many priests with pastoral experiences they valued and always remembered. Sharing the ministry of initiation should not deprive the priest of these meaningful opportunities. On the contrary, the Church looks to the parish priest to be available for pastoral counsel to catechumens and candidates as well as to sponsors, godparents, catechists, and others who may be sharing in the outreach to future Catholics.

Settling for "private instructions," however, deprives a candidate or cate-chumen of a full exposure to the Catholic community and its lived faith.

Deacons

Deacons are closely associated with priests in the ministry of initiation (see RCIA, 13, 15). They may preside at some of the initiation rites and preach. In those areas where priests are not available, the deacon may be expected to assume some of the responsibilities ordinarily assigned to the parish priest, including responsibility for overseeing the full process of the order of Christian initiation.

Permanent deacons may be well suited for introducing candidates and catechumens to works of charity and justice. A deacon also may serve as one of the catechists if he has been trained in adult catechesis.

In general, the deacon's involvement will depend on local need and on his own gifts. Ordinarily, however, a deacon should not act as sponsor or godparent. Rather, his ministry to those being initiated should be focused more broadly. As already mentioned regarding the pastor's role, the deacon should not be the only catechist or resort to private instructions even if there is only one candidate or catechumen.

Liturgists and Musicians

Because the liturgy is so integral to the order of initiation, liturgists and musicians should rightly be drawn into the parish's initiation ministry. Rites that will take place within the Sunday assembly should be prepared with the assistance of the liturgists and musicians so that the rites are integrated into the overall liturgical life of the community. If the liturgical rites are poorly prepared, understanding of their meaning and significance may be diminished. A weak, unconnected rite will seem to be an interruption of the liturgy and annoy the congregation rather than involve them in this important dynamic of the Church's life.

Because music is such an integral part of the liturgy, musicians should work closely with catechists to introduce music into the catechumens' and candidates' formation. Liturgical musicians can help catechumens and candidates discover spiritual and theological teaching contained in the musical texts and can help to prepare them for active and conscious participation in the liturgy. Liturgists and musicians can be a valuable resource in the preparations for prayer within the catechumenal sessions.

Spiritual Guides, Directors, or Companions

In many ways the entire process of Christian initiation can be viewed as spiritual direction. Pastors and catechumenal leaders have the awesome responsibility of accompanying others on the path to spiritual maturity. Through liturgical rites, spontaneous prayer, instruction, dialogue, and group activities, men and women are introduced into the Christian way of life and encouraged to develop their own vision of life and self that reflects the way of Jesus and the tradition of the Church.

Spiritual direction or accompaniment helps people discern what God wants of them in light of the Gospel.

While the potential for spiritual formation through participation in the catechumenal community should not be underestimated, one-on-one spiritual direction is also valuable. Individual spiritual direction allows a person the opportunity to focus on his or her own life and gifts to develop a personal response to the Christian mystery.

What is spiritual direction? The definition offered by Katherine Dyckman and L. Patrick Carroll is helpful:

Spiritual direction [is] an interpersonal relationship in which one person assists others to reflect on their own experience in the light of who they are called to become in fidelity to the gospel.[11]

11. Katherine Marie Dyckman, SNJM, and L. Patrick Carroll, SJ. *Inviting the Mystic, Supporting the Prophet* (New York: Paulist Press, 1981), 20.

Spiritual direction or accompaniment helps people discern what God wants of them in light of the Gospel. The spiritual guide does not tell one what to do or how to do it, but rather assists one to recognize the voice of God in his or her own life. The spiritual guide is a mentor, a companion, a facilitator. A good spiritual companion recognizes the need to listen to the Spirit in his or her own life. He or she knows the struggle of faith and prayer and is a good listener. The goal of spiritual accompaniment is to help a brother or sister to develop a healthy, mature spirituality. The definition of spirituality by Fr. Anscar Chupungco, osb, is helpful for understanding the larger goal of the spiritual process in the catechumenate:

> Spirituality is the endeavor to discover the face of God in the daily routine of life at home, in school, or place of employment. It is the ability to find peace of mind and contentment of heart in one's world and enjoy it to the full. . . . Spiritual people blend all aspects of life so that they can form a harmonious unity. They live an integrated life that has no compartments separating one life experience from another. There is no dichotomy between their prayer and their work or the performance of one's daily tasks, as if these realities were estranged from one another. For holistic persons everything leads to God and everything becomes a factor of growth in the spiritual life.[12]

The ministry of spiritual direction or companionship is not reserved to clergy or religious. Whoever is chosen ought to receive some training, but that person must first be a faithful and mature person. Those chosen for this ministry should be meeting regularly with their own spiritual directors or companions.

The spiritual companion or director need not be a regular participant in the catechumenate sessions. It will be preferable if they are not part of the catechumenate team that assesses the candidate's readiness for the initiation sacraments. Spiritual directors or guides do not judge those whom they direct, nor are they free to divulge the content of their conversations.

Catechumens and candidates are not obliged to choose a spiritual director, but they should know who is available to assist them.

---

12. Anscar J. Chupungco, osb, *What, Then, Is Liturgy? Musings and Memoir* (Collegeville, MN: Liturgical Press, 2010), 234–235.

Hospitality

The ministry of hospitality can set the tone for the entire initiation process. Opening doors, arranging the room, setting out coffee and cookies, welcoming people as they arrive—these simple actions let people know they are welcome and cared for. Responsibility for hospitality could be shared among the organizations of the parish or any parishioners who are interested in doing their part in the initiation of new members and who have a gift of welcoming others with a friendly spirit.

———— ◆ ————

Questions for Discussion and Reflection

1. How has your faith been influenced and supported by others?

2. How does your parish community welcome, support, and give witness to inquirers, candidates, and catechumens?

3. What are some of the ways you can encourage and recruit new members for your catechumenate team?

4. Knowing the scope of responsibility entrusted to an initiation team, what kind of ongoing formation for your parish team is appropriate?

5. What other ministries might you imagine could be included on the initiation team?

———— ◆ ————

CHAPTER FIVE

FREQUENTLY ASKED QUESTIONS

1. Who are today's inquirers?

Many people today are searching for meaning and hope in a world that can strike us as being confusing, divided, and uninspiring. Some become seekers, looking for meaning and direction. Some have become disillusioned with institutional religion. You may hear them saying they are "spiritual" but not "religious," which means they aren't committed to any particular church or religious institution. The 2014 Pew Research group reported that 35 percent of millennials (18–35 years old) claimed no religious affiliation (referred to as NONES). While the Catholic population in the United States is listed as 20.8 percent of the total population, 12.9 percent of Americans claim to be former Catholics. Out of these demographics we can presume that there is a fertile field for evangelization. The difficulty is that those we might term "seekers" do not immediately turn to the Church to satisfy their quest for meaning and spiritual depth. This is the challenge every parish has to face if we want to see seekers become inquirers.

The work of evangelization complements the work of initiation. Our outreach to seekers is best accomplished by Catholic parishioners who value their faith and recognize that they are called to be missionary disciples who are the first point of contact with seekers. It takes a personal invitation to begin the process of exploring what the Church has to offer. We often hear from inquirers, "I would have come to the Church sooner, but no one ever asked me if I was interested."

Many inquirers are interested in becoming Christians or members of the Catholic Church because someone in their family, perhaps a spouse, has been a source of inspiration and encouragement to them. Work associates or a faith-filled neighbor may be the catalyst that stirs the soul of a future inquirer.

A vital parish with good liturgy and preaching, a welcoming community, and a reputation for caring about others can attract those who are looking for a spiritual home. Parishes that have a good sense of mission, reaching out into the neighborhood to the poor, the immigrant, the single parent, the unemployed, to young adults, and so on, will attract men and women who will be open to discovering the Good News of Jesus in the local parish.

2. How do we minister to someone who is preparing to marry soon and would like to be initiated before the wedding?

Christian initiation and Christian Marriage are two separate and important decisions in a person's life. Each is a call, a vocation given by God, and each must be responded to freely and without undue haste.

The desire of the non-Catholic party to enter the full communion of the Catholic Church has to be handled sensitively. If the couple is preparing to marry before the non-Catholic partner is ready to be baptized or received into full communion, it is better to obtain the appropriate dispensation allowing the Catholic party to marry an unbaptized person or a baptized person of another Christian tradition. If the inquirer is genuinely interested in the Christian initiation process, then he or she can enter the catechumenate after the wedding. The individual may also begin the process before the wedding, knowing that he or she will not be baptized or received until sometime after it. Being baptized or received into the full communion of the

A non-Catholic seeking initiation may begin the process before the wedding, knowing that he or she will not be baptized or received until sometime after it.

Catholic Church for the convenience of a scheduled wedding date will not ordinarily allow for sufficient time for the conversion process to mature and do justice to all that the catechumenate tries to achieve.

There are exceptions, of course. A baptized, catechized, practicing member of another Christian tradition, or, more rarely, an unbaptized person who has been catechized and formed in the faith may need very little spiritual formation and thus could be baptized or received before the wedding. This is a pastoral judgment that should not be taken lightly but requires an honest assessment of what will be best suited for an individual. The RCIA sees initiation not as an obstacle course, but as pastoral care for each individual, and so it is flexible. At the same time flexibility should not become an excuse for sacrificing the integrity of the initiation process.

If the non-Catholic party has not been baptized or received before the wedding takes place, the couple should be assured that their marriage will be valid in the Catholic Church. If the non-Catholic party is validly baptized, the Marriage is considered sacramental at the time of the wedding. In the case of an unbaptized bride or groom, the marriage will be considered sacramental after the unbaptized party is baptized. They will not need to remake their vows after the non-Catholic partner is baptized or received.

3. Can we initiate someone who is in a canonically irregular marriage?

Anyone who is being initiated into the Church must be free to celebrate the sacraments. Very early in the initiation process the marital status of the inquirer should be ascertained through a personal interview. If an annulment is required by the Church, that process should begin immediately. Participation in the initiation process has to be weighed carefully. It may be wise to delay formal participation in the parish catechumenate. Otherwise the individual becomes attached to the catechumenate community with the expectation of being initiated with everyone else at the next Easter celebration. On the other hand, a pastoral decision may be made to include the inquirer in the evangelization stage with the clear understanding that they may not be initiated with the rest of the group. Support for the inquirer through spiritual direction and sponsorship should be expected during this time. Once the canonical marriage has been resolved, the individual is free to proceed with the complete process of initiation.

If a community judges that it is pastorally advantageous to include men and women whose canonical marital status has yet to be resolved, those men and women may participate in the catechumenate but will not participate in the Rite of Election.

4. Is the Easter Vigil the only time the sacraments of initiation may be celebrated?

From very early times the Church has seen Easter as a most appropriate time for Christian initiation, for it is through the sacraments of initiation that

we are freed from the power of darkness and joined to Christ's death, burial, and resurrection. We receive the Spirit of filial adoption and are part of the entire people of God in the celebration of the memorial of the Lord's death and resurrection.[1]

When it is necessary to initiate new members outside the Easter Vigil (perhaps because their formation could not be completed by then), a date during Easter Time (such as the Solemnity of Pentecost) is preferred because of the integral connection to the Paschal Mystery. Even a date outside of Easter Time should carry the meaning of the Lord's Death and Resurrection. Outside of Easter Time, selecting a Sunday such as the Feast of the Baptism of the Lord or the Solemnity of Our Lord Jesus Christ, King of the Universe may be suitable.[2]

The Rite of Reception into the Full Communion of the Catholic Church should preferably take place at another time outside the Easter Vigil, especially when there are Baptisms being celebrated at the Vigil. The Rite of Reception can be celebrated at any time during the year and is dependent primarily upon the readiness of the individual. Candidates for reception into full communion should not be held back arbitrarily, waiting perhaps months before Easter.[3]

The Rite of Reception into the Full Communion of the Catholic Church should preferably take place at another time outside the Easter Vigil, especially when there are Baptisms being celebrated at the Vigil.

---

1. *Christian Initiation*, General Introduction, 1.
2. If, for pastoral reasons, the sacraments of initiation do not take place at the Easter Vigil, use the texts "For the Conferral of Baptism" as found in the third edition of *The Roman Missal* on days in which Ritual Masses are permitted.
3. On days in which Ritual Masses are permitted, the texts "For the Conferral of Confirmation" from the third edition of *The Roman Missal* may be used.

5. When is it appropriate to celebrate the Sacrament of Penance?

Since all sin is remitted in Baptism, those who are preparing for Baptism do not celebrate the Sacrament of Penance before they are initiated. Catechumens should, however, be catechized about the Sacrament of Penance and be encouraged to celebrate the sacrament at a later time.

For candidates preparing to be received into full communion, the most suitable time to celebrate this sacrament would be during Lent if they are going to be received into the Church in Easter Time. The Sacrament of Penance can serve, as some early Church writers such as St. Ambrose have called it, "a second baptism, the first in water and second tears." The celebration of the Sacrament of Penance gives the candidate an opportunity to review their life, confess their sins, and accept the merciful forgiveness of God as they begin to walk a new path in faith. Outside the Lent / Easter cycle, it is appropriate to celebrate the Sacrament of Penance after the candidate is prepared and feels ready to submit themselves to the mercy and forgiveness of God.

The celebration of the Sacrament of Penance gives the candidates an opportunity to review their life, confess their sins, and accept the merciful forgiveness of God as they begin to walk a new path in faith.

The support of sponsors may be helpful to candidates as they celebrate this sacrament for the first time. They may wish to accompany them to the church and, perhaps, prepare for the sacrament together. Because many non-Catholics often have been given a poor impression of reconciliation (even by Catholics), it is important for the sponsor to approach this sacrament positively and with joy.

The general norms for reconciliation apply to the baptized candidates: No one can be obliged to celebrate the Sacrament of Reconciliation except for serious sin (see RCIA, 482). If they have been catechized well and have had the opportunity to resolve their fears or misunderstandings, most candidates will want to celebrate the sacrament.

6. If Christians being received into the full communion of the Catholic Church have already been confirmed in another denomination, do we confirm them again?

The Catholic Church confirms baptized Christians when they are received into full communion. While other Christian churches may celebrate the presence of the Holy Spirit in the life of a person who is maturing in faith, Roman Catholics believe that Confirmation is one of the seven sacraments instituted by Christ for the Church. In other words, even if there are Christian Churches who use the term *Confirmation*, it does not mean the same thing as it does for Catholics. With Baptism and Eucharist, the Sacrament of Confirmation is necessary to be fully initiated into the Catholic Church.

7. Does this apply to those who are entering the Roman Catholic Church from the Orthodox Church?

No. Orthodox Christians share the same seven sacraments as Roman Catholics. An Orthodox Christian who has been confirmed (called receiving "chrismation" in Orthodox Churches) enters into the Catholic Church by making a profession of faith.

8. What if new inquirers approach the parish long after the Period of the Precatechumenate has begun?

The Holy Spirit may lead people to our doors at any time of the year. Regardless of the time, they should be warmly welcomed. After a personal interview, they may be included in the precatechumenate and evangelization group. Because the agenda for the precatechumenate is shaped by the needs of the inquirers, there should be little difficulty integrating the new inquirer into the group. No one should ever be turned away or told to come back in several months.

Ideally the Period of the Precatechumenate and Evangelization will be available all year round. Perhaps a family or group of individuals can take responsibility for a weekly open-door precatechumenate. When individuals are ready to move on to the catechumenate, they simply join the catechumenate group whenever it meets. The catechumenate group also would meet year-round, presumably after being dismissed after Sunday's Liturgy of the Word.

9. Can a college campus be the setting for a catechumenal process?

The college years often are a time for questioning the meaning and purpose of one's life. Students look to the future and seek hope and direction. These are years of exploration, testing old assumptions, looking for answers to questions that were never asked before. The college years can be the ripe moment for a new evangelization.

Where there is an active Newman Center or Catholic presence on campus, college students may discover that the Church has a great deal to offer them. Some may not have been raised in a religious environment. Others may have a religious background but until now never took it seriously.

College-centered catechumenate groups may encounter difficulty when the school year calendar is out of sync with the liturgical year. The initiation process is intended to culminate at the Easter Vigil, but at some schools the Triduum coincides with spring break. In these instances the sacraments of initiation may best be celebrated on the Second or Third Sunday of Easter or on the Solemnity of Pentecost. The initiation sacraments would not be celebrated during Lent.

Other pastoral concerns that arise for a campus-centered catechumenal process are the period of mystagogy and integration into a parish community. Catechumenal teams will need to develop a support system for the newly initiated that can continue beyond campus life. Guidance in choosing a sponsor who will be able to maintain contact would be wise.

Communication with pastors where the newly initiated make their home will help provide a supportive link.

10. What if someone's psychological or emotional needs are greater than the catechumenal process can fulfill?

It is not uncommon that individuals searching for psychological or emotional wholeness will look in many directions for peace of mind. They may look to religion for the answer to their problems or anxieties.

While we believe that religious faith does help us to live a peaceful and integrated life, sometimes psychological needs overpower all else and must be addressed professionally before participation in a catechumenal community is advised. The catechumenal community is not a therapy group, but rather presumes the participation of mature and healthy adults.

Interviews prior to participation in the catechumenal group will be very important for surfacing any serious psychological or emotional issues. When these problems arise in the interviews or in the group, the individual should be encouraged to seek professional help. Even though he or she may not be taken immediately into the catechumenal community, the pastoral team still can maintain a pastoral relationship and keep close contact with the individual. This situation requires great sensitivity. Parish teams should discuss the possibility of such a situation arising and how they will address it.

11. Can we use the RCIA as a renewal program for Catholics?

Christian communities need to be committed to ongoing renewal. However, the RCIA is designed for those who are preparing for the sacraments of initiation. If the rite is used for everyone, its impact and its unique character may be diluted. The background, the questions, and the relationship with the Church is going to be significantly different for the Catholic looking for renewal compared to catechumens and candidates encountering Christ in their life for the first time and discovering the foundations of Church life.

Nevertheless, there is much we can learn from the RCIA that can be applied in caring for the spiritual renewal of a community. In particular, the dynamics of evangelization, conversion, sponsorship, ritual prayer, and apostolic involvement may give shape to a parish's renewal efforts. Whether in small groups or as a larger group process, parishioners can be led through a process of spiritual formation that is distinct from the formal catechumenate but inspired by the same dynamics.

When a community walks through the liturgical year with catechumens and candidates and observes Lent, the Sacred Paschal Triduum, and Easter Time in all their fullness, the community will have the opportunity to experience a genuine spirit of renewal.

12. Why are we discouraged from calling our parish Catechumenate "RCIA Classes"?

The preparation of adults for the initiation sacraments is a ritual process that includes spiritual formation, a series of rites, evangelization, catechesis, engagement with the parish community, an introduction to missionary discipleship, and a period of mystagogy to delve deeper in the experience of the Christian mystery. This is clearly not a "class." A *class* refers to an academic program with specific start and end dates. A *class* implies acquiring a specific amount of information—in this situation official Church teaching. To refer to "RCIA Classes" is misleading because it does not convey the holistic pastoral approach as outlined in the RCIA for initiating individuals into Christ and his Church.

13. Can the RCIA be accommodated to the school calendar?

As noted in question 12, the process of Christian initiation is not a class with a syllabus. Christian initiation respects the human dimensions of life and faith, which require flexibility. Adequate time must be allowed for conversion to mature, for faith to be nurtured by catechesis, and for relationships to develop. Predetermining the length of the initiation process by artificially structuring a schedule to fit the school year would fail to respect the unique journey of faith.

14. How can a small parish develop a strong catechumenate?

While a small parish may be limited by the number of parishioners available to form a catechumenal team, the entire parish can be considered the catechumenal community. Inquirers, candidates (for the catechumenate), and catechumens may more easily be integrated into the community's life and mission. The key is not to resort to private instructions because it may be more convenient. Every inquirer, candidate (for the catechumenate), or catechumen deserves the support and mentoring of a community, not just one person. In some cases a small parish may be near another parish with the same pastor. In these situations some of the catechetical formation may be offered in one place. The various rites, however, should still be celebrated in the community where the individual is planning to call their spiritual home.

15. How do we tell an individual that he or she is not ready to move to the next stage or be initiated?

The initiation process presumes ongoing dialogue with a member of the parish initiation team and also a sponsor. If open conversations are taking place, there should be no surprises. Ideally, the candidate or catechumen will discern whether he or she is ready for the next step. Discernment for readiness is not a test like we might take in a class. Discernment includes listening to the heart, looking for signs of spiritual change, a growing commitment to Christ and his Church, and so on. The wording we find in the liturgical rites—for example, the inquiry made to godparents and assembly (see RCIA, 131)—offer insight into what we are hoping to find in a candidate or catechumenate who is ready for the initiation sacraments.

16. What do we do when a question is raised for which we do not know the answer?

When a catechumenate team is presented with a question no one on the team can answer, it presents a good learning situation for how one continues to grow in faith. It may be comforting for a candidate or catechumen to see that even their Catholic mentors don't know everything. The team, however, should find the answer. A team should take the question raised and suggest some research options. The team might look into the *Catechism of the Catholic Church* or a reliable website, or someone on parish staff who can help.

APPENDIX A

PERIODS AND STEPS IN THE RITE OF CHRISTIAN INITIATION OF ADULTS

	First Period	First Step	Second Period
	Period of Evangelization and Precatechumenate	Rite of Acceptance into the Order of Catechumens	Period of the Catechumenate
Time	Indefinite length	When inquirer and community discern readiness	Year (including Period of Purification and Enlightenment)
Name	**Inquirer**		**Catechumen**
What occurs during this period or step	Proclamation of the Gospel and Jesus Christ, leading to faith and initial conversion; introduction to the Christian community	Inquirers publicly declare their intention to become members of the Church; Church accepts them as catechumens.	Formation through catechesis, experience of the Christian way of life through familiarity with community, participation in the liturgical life of the community, and participation in the apostolic life of the Church
Rites belonging to the period	No formal rites; individual prayers and blessings may take place as appropriate.		Celebrations of the Word, Blessings, Anointings, Minor Exorcisms

Second Step	Third Period	Third Step	Fourth Period
Rite of Election	Period of Purification and Enlightenment	Celebration of Sacraments of Initiation	Period of Mystagogy
First Sunday of Lent	Lent	Easter Vigil	Easter Time; extended Mystagogy for one year
	Elect		**Neophyte**
In the name of the Church, the bishop judges readiness of catechumens for initiation and declares that they are chosen for sacraments at the next Easter Vigil.	Retreat-like preparation for the celebration of sacraments of initiation	Initiation into the Church through Baptism, Confirmation, and Eucharist	Deepening of understanding of Paschal Mystery through meditation on the Gospel, participation in the Eucharist, and doing works of charity.
	Scrutinies, Presentations of the Creed and Lord's Prayer, Preparatory Rites on Holy Saturday		Sunday Masses of Easter Time; celebrations near Pentecost and anniversary of initiation; Mass with the bishop

APPENDIX B

OUTLINES OF THE RITES OF CHRISTIAN INITIATION OF ADULTS

The Rite of Acceptance into the Order of Catechumens

RCIA, 41–68

Receiving the Candidates

- Greeting
- Opening Dialogue
- Candidates' First Acceptance of the Gospel
- Affirmation by the Sponsors and the Assembly
- Signing of the Candidates with the Cross
  - Signing of the Forehead
  - [Signing of the Other Senses]
  - Concluding Prayer
- Invitation to the Celebration of the Word of God

Liturgy of the Word

- Instruction
- Readings
- Homily
- [Presentation of a Bible]
- Intercessions for the Catechumens
- Prayer over the Catechumens
- Dismissal of the Catechumens

Liturgy of the Eucharist

Rite of Welcoming the Candidates

RCIA, 411–433

Welcoming the Candidates

- Greeting
- Opening Dialogue
- Candidates' Declaration of Intent
- Affirmation by the Sponsors and the Assembly
- Signing of the Candidates with the Cross
  - Signing of the Forehead
  - [Signing of the Other Senses]
  - Concluding Prayer

Liturgy of the Word

- Instruction
- Readings
- Homily
- [Presentation of a Bible]
- Profession of Faith
- General Intercessions
- Prayer over the Candidates
- [Dismissal of the Assembly]

Liturgy of the Eucharist

Rite of Election or Enrollment of Names

RCIA, 118–137

Liturgy of the Word

- Homily
- Presentation of the Catechumens
- Affirmation by the Godparents [and the Assembly]
- Invitation and Enrollment of Names
- Act of Admission or Election
- Intercessions for the Elect
- Prayer over the Elect
- Dismissal of the Elect

Liturgy of the Eucharist

Rite of Calling the Candidates to Continuing Conversion

RCIA, 446–458

Liturgy of the Word

- Homily
- Presentation of the Candidates for Confirmation and Eucharist
- Affirmation by the Sponsors [and the Assembly]
- Act of Recognition
- General Intercessions
- Prayer over the Candidates
- [Dismissal of the Assembly]

Liturgy of the Eucharist

The First, Second, and Third Scrutinies

RCIA, 141–156, 164–170, and 171–177

Liturgy of the Word

- Readings
- Homily
- Invitation to Silent Prayer
- Intercessions for the Elect
- Exorcism
- Dismissal of the Elect

Liturgy of the Eucharist

Penitential Rite (Scrutiny)

RCIA, 459–472

Introductory Rites

- Greeting and Introduction
- Prayer

Liturgy of the Word

- Readings
- Homily
- Invitation to Silent Prayer
- Intercessions for the Candidates
- Prayer over the Candidates
- [Dismissal of the Assembly]

Liturgy of the Eucharist

Celebration of the Sacraments of Initiation

RCIA, 206–243; see also the texts as found in
The Roman Missal for the Easter Vigil.

Liturgy of Light (Lucernarium)

Liturgy of the Word

Liturgy of Baptism

- Presentation of the Candidates
- Invitation to Prayer
- Litany of the Saints
- Prayer over the Water
- Profession of Faith
  - Renunciation of Sin
  - Profession of Faith
- Baptism
- Explanatory Rites
  - [Anointing after Baptism]
  - [Clothing with a Baptismal Garment]
  - Presentation of a Lighted Candle

Celebration of Confirmation

- Invitation
- Laying on of Hands
- Anointing with Chrism

[Renewal of Baptismal Promises (at the Easter Vigil)]

- Invitation
- Renewal of Baptismal Promises
- Sprinkling with Baptismal Water
  - Renunciation of Sin
  - Profession of Faith

Liturgy of the Eucharist

GLOSSARY

Adult For the purpose of sacramental initiation, a person who has reached the age of reason (also called the age of discretion or catechetical age), usually regarded to be seven years of age, is an adult. A person who has reached that age is to be initiated into the Church according to the RCIA and receive the three sacraments of initiation together, although the catechesis should be adapted to the individual's needs. Before this age, the person is considered legally to be an infant and is baptized using the *Rite of Baptism for Children.*

Apostles' Creed The ancient baptismal statement of the Church's faith. The questions used in the celebration of Baptism correspond to the statements of the Apostles' Creed.

Baptismal Font A large vessel that holds the water used in the Baptism of infants and adults, either by immersion or infusion (pouring). The baptismal font is ideally located in a place that allows for full congregational participation.

Blessing Any prayer that praises and thanks God. In particular, *blessing* describes those prayers in which God is praised because of some person or object, and thus the individual or object becomes specially dedicated or sanctified because of the prayer of faith.

Book of the Elect A book into which the names of those catechumens who have been chosen, or elected, for initiation at the next Easter Vigil are inscribed at or before the Rite of Election.

Book of the Gospels A ritual book from which the passages from the accounts of the Gospel prescribed for Masses on Sundays, solemnities and feasts of the Lord, and solemnities of the saints are proclaimed; also called an "evangeliary."

Candidate Generally, anyone preparing to become a Catholic, but the term is often used to denote a person baptized in another Christian tradition who is preparing for reception into the full communion of the Catholic Church.

Canon Law The body of law that governs Church practice and protects the rights and privileges of individuals and of the community.

Catechesis The instruction and spiritual formation of catechumens, neophytes, and those persons who seek full communion with the Catholic Church.

Catechetical Age Usually considered to be about seven years of age; also called the "age of reason" or the "age of discretion." For the purpose of Christian initiation, a person who has reached catechetical age is considered an adult and is to be initiated into the Church according to the RCIA.

Catechumen An unbaptized person who is seeking initiation into the Church and who has been accepted into the Order of Catechumens.

Catechumenate The process by which the Catholic Church brings unbaptized adults and children of catechetical age to Christian initiation.

Child For the purposes of Christian initiation, one who has not yet reached the age of reason (presumed to be about seven years of age) and who therefore cannot independently profess personal faith.

Chrism A combination of oil and sweet balsam or perfume that is mixed and consecrated by the bishop and used to anoint the newly baptized and newly ordained priests and bishops. Chrism is also used in the consecration of churches and altars.

Companion In the Christian initiation process with children of catechetical age, a baptized child of an age similar to the child catechumen who takes part in the catechetical group and accompanies the catechumen in the rites.

Dismissal The final, formal invitation by the deacon or, in his absence, the priest for the assembly to go forth from the liturgical celebration. The word can also refer to the dismissal of the catechumens after the homily at Mass.

Doctrine The formal teachings of the Church in matters of faith and morals.

Easter Vigil The Easter Vigil takes place the night before Easter Sunday. While the Church keeps watch this night, a fire is lighted, Scriptures are read that tell the story of salvation, the elect receive the Easter sacraments, and all present renew their baptismal promises.

Elect A catechumen who has been found ready by the community of faith to take part in the next celebration of the sacraments of initiation.

Election The process of selecting those catechumens who are considered ready to take part in the next celebration of the sacraments of initiation; the celebration ordinarily takes place on the First Sunday of Lent, wherein the bishop or his delegate declares in the name of the Church that particular catechumens are ready and chosen for the sacraments at Easter. During this celebration, the names of the elect are written in the Book of the Elect.

Enlightenment The period of Lent during which the elect are involved in the final stage of preparation for celebrating the rites of initiation. *Synonyms*: illumination, purification.

Enrollment The rite of inscribing into the Book of the Elect the names of those catechumens elected to take part in the next celebration of the sacraments of initiation. *See* election.

Ephphetha An optional rite in which the presider touches the ears and the mouth of the elect and prays that they be open to hear and proclaim the Word of God in faith. It may be celebrated as part of the preparation rites on Holy Saturday.

Evangelization The activity by which the Church proclaims the Gospel in word or in deed.

Exorcisms Prayers for the deliverance from the powers of evil and falsehood, and for the reception of the gifts of the Lord, especially the gifts of the Holy Spirit. Exorcisms are part of the scrutiny rites.

Fasting A form of sacrifice by which faithful Christians join themselves with the suffering and Death of Jesus by forgoing food for a specific period of time. On Ash Wednesday and Good Friday, Catholics who are in good health and between the ages of 18 and 59 (inclusive) are obliged to fast in a modified way: One full meal and two other small meals may be eaten, and no food is eaten between meals. Catholics are encouraged to keep a paschal fast from Holy Thursday evening until after the Easter Vigil in anticipation of the celebration of the Lord's resurrection.

Faculty A right granted to enable a person to do something, usually referring to a right granted to a priest or deacon by law or by the bishop.

Godparent The person who accompanies the catechumen during the rites and periods of election, initiation, and mystagogy. This person (or persons) is selected by the catechumen with the approval of the pastor and, when appropriate, in collaboration with the initiation ministers.

Holy Saturday The Saturday within the Sacred Paschal Triduum. It is a day marked by meditation, prayer, and fasting in anticipation of the Resurrection of the Lord. Several Preparation Rites for the elect who will be receiving the sacraments of initiation at the Vigil are proper to this day.

Illumination *See* enlightenment.

Immersion A way of baptizing in which the person is partially or entirely submerged in the baptismal water.

Infusion A way of baptizing in which the baptismal water is poured over the head of the candidate.

Inquirer An unbaptized adult who sincerely seeks to learn about the faith of the Church.

Inquiry Another name given to the Period of Evangelization and Precatechumenate, the first period or stage in the process of Christian initiation.

Initiation The process by which a person enters the faith life of the Church—from the catechumenate through the normally continuous celebration of the sacramental rites of Baptism, Confirmation, and Eucharist. The process extends from the person's first inquiry through the completion of mystagogy.

Laying on of Hands A gesture of blessing or invocation recorded in the New Testament in conjunction with prayer (for example, Acts of the Apostles 13:3; 2 Timothy 1:6). The gesture is performed by extending both hands forward with the palms turned downward. Depending on the circumstances, the hands may be placed on the person's head or stretched out over a group of people or over an object.

Lectionary-based catechesis A catechetical method for learning the foundation of faith and doctrine by study of and reflection on the Scriptures as they are arranged for the liturgy over a three-year cycle.

Lectionary for Mass A book containing the assigned Scripture readings for the celebration of the Eucharist and the other sacraments.

Litany of Saints A litany that calls upon the saints to pray for the Church, believed to be the most ancient litany in the Church's worship.

Liturgy of the Hours A form of prayer consisting of Scripture, psalms, and prayers for morning, daytime, evening, and nighttime of each solemnity, feast, memorial, season, Sunday, and weekday.

Magisterium The official teaching office of the Church as it is exercised by the pope in communion with all the bishops of the Church.

Minor Rites Rites during the catechumenate, which include the Rite of Exorcism, Rite of Blessing, and Rite of Anointing.

Mystagogy The period following initiation, usually Easter Time, which centers on catechesis in the meaning and experience of the mysteries of baptismal faith.

National Statutes for the Catechumenate A document issued by the National Conference of Catholic Bishops (now the United States Conference of Catholic Bishops) in 1986, and confirmed by the Apostolic See in 1988, constituting particular law for the implementation of the RCIA in the United States.

Neophyte A newly baptized person who is in the final period of Christian initiation, mystagogy.

Oil of Catechumens The blessed oil used in anointing catechumens as a sign of their need for God's strength in overcoming all opposition to the faith they will profess throughout their life.

Order of Catechumens The canonical group to which an unbaptized adult who is preparing to receive the sacraments of initiation belongs after celebrating the Rite of Acceptance into the Order of Catechumens.

Order of Christian Initiation The progression of catechesis and rituals that make up the process of bringing a person to faith in Christ and membership in the Church. The term sometimes refers to the text used for initiation, *Rite of Christian Initiation of Adults*.

Paschal Candle The large candle lighted each year from the new fire ignited and blessed at the Easter Vigil. From this light, representing the Risen Lord who destroys the darkness of sin, the newly baptized light their candles. Also commonly referred to as the Easter candle.

Paschal Mystery The saving mystery of Christ's life, Passion, Death, and Resurrection. It is the mystery that is celebrated and made present in every liturgy, and the mystery that every Christian is to imitate and identify with in everyday life.

Postbaptismal Catechesis Mystagogical catechesis given to the newly baptized, or neophytes, to help them deepen their understanding of the faith primarily through reflection on the sacraments they celebrated at Easter.

Precatechumenate A period of indeterminate length that precedes acceptance into the Order of Catechumens. In the RCIA, this time is called the Period of Evangelization and Precatechumenate; it is also referred to as "inquiry."

Preparation Rites Various rites that can be celebrated with the elect on Holy Saturday in proximate preparation for the celebration of the sacraments of initiation at the Easter Vigil that evening.

Presentations Rites whereby the Church entrusts the Creed and the Lord's Prayer, the ancient texts that express the heart of the Church's faith and prayer tradition to the elect.

Purification and Enlightenment The period of final preparation for unbaptized adults journeying toward initiation in the Catholic Church. It is a time of intense spiritual preparation marked by the celebration of the scrutinies, presentations, and the traditional disciplines of Lent.

RCIA Abbreviation of *Rite of Christian Initiation of Adults*, the official rite of the Roman Catholic Church that includes the norms, directives, and ritual celebrations for initiating unbaptized adults and children who have reached catechetical age into Christ and incorporating them into the Church. The RCIA prescribes a sequence of periods and rites by which candidates transition from one stage to another, culminating in the celebration of the sacraments at the Easter Vigil.

Reception of Baptized Christians into the Full Communion of the Catholic Church The liturgical rite for receiving into the full communion of the Catholic Church an adult who was validly baptized in a non-Catholic Christian community.

Register of Catechumens The book in which the names of those unbaptized adults who have been accepted as catechumens are recorded. The names of the sponsors and the minister and the date and place of the celebration of the Rite of Acceptance into the Order of Catechumens should also be recorded. Each parish should maintain a Register of Catechumens.

Renunciation of Sins The ritual questioning that precedes the Profession of Faith made at Baptism or in the Renewal of Baptismal Promises. There are two alternative forms of the formula for the renunciation of sin, each of which consists of three questions that center on the rejection of Satan and his works.

Rite of Acceptance into the Order of Catechumens The formal beginning of the initiation process for the unbaptized.

Rite of Election The second step for unbaptized adults preparing for the sacraments of initiation, also called the "Enrollment of Names." The rite closes the Period of the Catechumenate and marks the beginning of the Period of Purification and Enlightenment, which usually corresponds to Lent. With this rite, the Church makes her election, or choice, of the catechumens to receive the sacraments. The Rite of Election normally takes place on or near the First Sunday of Lent.

The Roman Missal The ritual book including the prayers, antiphons, and Scripture readings prescribed for the celebration of Mass. The present day Missal, currently in its third edition, is divided into several books, the central of which are the book of prayers and rubrics used by the priest, called *The Roman Missal* (although it contains only these parts of the full Missal) and the *Lectionary for Mass*, which includes the Scripture readings.

Sacred Paschal Triduum The three days from Holy Thursday evening through Easter Sunday evening that celebrate the Passover of Israel from slavery to freedom, the Passover of Jesus Christ from death to life, our own Passover from sin to grace, and the world's Passover from darkness to light.

Scrutinies Rites celebrated with the elect, usually at Sunday Mass on the Third, Fourth, and Fifth Sundays of Lent, petitioning for the spirit of repentance, an understanding of sin, and the experience of the true freedom of the children of God.

Sending of the Catechumens for Election An optional rite that may be celebrated before the catechumens take part in the Rite of Election. The rite, which usually takes place at Mass, expresses the parish community's approval and support of the catechumens' election by the bishop.

Sponsors Those persons who accompany the inquirers when they seek acceptance into the Order of Catechumens and who remain with them as companions during the catechumenate until the Rite of Election, when godparents begin to accompany the elect and the candidates to the Easter sacraments.

White Garment The clothing, similar to an alb, which is given to someone immediately after Baptism. This garment is a sign that the newly baptized person has put on new life in Christ. It is used in the Baptism of both adults and children.